Indigenous Australians and the National Disability Insurance Scheme

Indigenous Australians and the National Disability Insurance Scheme

N. Biddle, F. Al-Yaman, M. Gourley, M. Gray, J. R. Bray,
B. Brady, L. A. Pham, E. Williams, M. Montaigne

Australian
National
University

PRESS

Centre for Aboriginal Economic Policy Research
College of Arts and Social Sciences
The Australian National University, Canberra

Research Monograph No. 34

2014

ANU PRESS

Published by ANU Press
The Australian National University
Canberra ACT 0200, Australia
Email: anupress@anu.edu.au
This title is also available online at http://press.anu.edu.au

---

National Library of Australia Cataloguing-in-Publication entry

Author: Biddle, Nicholas, author.

Title: Indigenous Australians and the National Disability
                Insurance Scheme / N. Biddle, F.
                Al-Yaman, M. Gourley, M. Gray, J. R.
                Bray, B. Brady, L. A. Pham, E.
                Williams, M. Montaigne.

ISBN: 9781925021882 (paperback) 9781925021899 (ebook)

Subjects: National Disability Insurance Scheme (Australia)
                Aboriginal Australians with disabilities--Services
                for--Australia.
                Aboriginal Australians with disabilities--Care--Australia.
                Aboriginal Australians with disabilities--Government
                policy--Australia.
                Long-term care insurance--Law and legislation--Australia.

Other Authors/Contributors:

                Al-Yaman, Fadwa, author.
                Gourley, Michelle, author.
                Gray, M, author.
                Bray, J. R., author.
                Brady, B., author.
                Pham, L. A., author.
                Williams, E., author.
                Montaigne, M., author.

Dewey Number: 362.10994

Cover design by Nic Welbourn and layout by ANU Press

Contents

List of Figures

List of Tables

Abbreviations and acronyms

ABS	Australian Bureau of Statistics
ADHC	Ageing, Disability and Home Care (New South Wales)
AIHW	Australian Institute of Health and Welfare
ANAO	Australian National Audit Office
ATSIC	Aboriginal and Torres Strait Islander Commission
ATSIS	Aboriginal and Torres Strait Islander Services
CAEPR	Centre for Aboriginal Economic Policy Research
CDEP	Community Development Employment Projects
CGC	Commonwealth Grants Commission
COAG	Council of Australian Governments
CSTDA	Commonwealth State/Territory Disability Agreement
DIG	Disability Investment Group
DSS	Department of Social Services
DS NMDS	Disability Services National Minimum Data Set
ERP	Estimated Resident Population
FaHCSIA	Department of Families, Housing, Community Services and Indigenous Affairs
FNIHCC	First Nations and Inuit Home and Community Care
FPDN	First Peoples Disability Network
GSS	General Social Survey
HACC	Home and Community Aged Care
ICF	International Classification of Functioning, Disability and Health
ICSP	Individual Community Support Package
ISP	individual support package
IREG	Indigenous Region
NATSIHS	National Aboriginal and Torres Strait Islander Health Survey
NATSISS	National Aboriginal and Torres Strait Islander Social Survey
NDA	National Disability Agreement

NDIS	National Disability Insurance Scheme
NGO	non-government organisation
NHS	National Health Survey
NPARSD	National Partnership Agreement on Remote Service Delivery
RSDA	Remote Service Delivery Area
SCRGSP	Steering Committee for the Review of Government Service Provision
SDAC	Survey of Disability and Carers
SOW	Services Our Way
SLA	Statistical Local Area
UN	United Nations
YPIRAC	Younger People in Residential Aged Care

Acknowledgements

A draft version of this manuscript was reviewed by Professor Maggie Walter from the University of Tasmania and Dr John Gilroy from the University of Sydney, and their comments were greatly appreciated. In the process of developing this monograph a number of individuals and groups were consulted including Aboriginal Medical Services Alliances NT (AMSANT), Carpentaria Disability Services, Damian Griffis (First Peoples Disability Network), Anthony Hogan (ANU), Boyd Hunter (ANU), Sven Silburn (Menzies School of Health Research), and John Wakerman (Centre for Remote Health, Flinders University). Comments were also provided by officials from the then Commonwealth Department of Families, Housing, Community Services and Indigenous Affairs (FaHCSIA) and relevant State/Territory Departments. Research assistance was provided by Mandy Yap. Finally, expert editorial assistance was provided by Frances Morphy, Hilary Bek, Clare Brennan and John Hughes from CAEPR, as well as the very helpful staff from ANU Press.

Author affiliations

Nicholas Biddle is a Fellow at the Centre for Aboriginal Economic Policy Research at The Australian National University.

Fadwa Al-Yaman is Group Head, Social and Indigenous Group at the Australian Institute of Health and Welfare.

Michelle Gourley is Unit Head, Indigenous Data Analysis and Reporting Unit at the Australian Institute of Health and Welfare.

Matthew Gray is Director and Professor at the Centre for Aboriginal Economic Policy Research at The Australian National University, and Director of Research in the College of Arts and Social Science at The Australian National University.

J. Rob Bray was a Research Fellow at the Research School of Economics and is now a Research Fellow at the Centre for Aboriginal Economic Policy Research at The Australian National University.

Brendan Brady is Project Manager/ Senior Data Analyst, Functioning and Disability Unit at the Australian Institute of Health and Welfare.

Le Anh Pham is Project Manager, Health Performance Framework Report Project at the Australian Institute of Health and Welfare.

Emma Williams is a Visiting Fellow at the Centre for Aboriginal Economic Policy Research at The Australian National University.

Maxine Montaigne was a Research Officer at the Centre for Aboriginal Economic Policy at The Australian National University and is currently a PhD Student in Economic Research History at the London School of Economics.

1. Introduction: Developing the National Disability Insurance Scheme

The Australian Government is in the process of developing a National Disability Insurance Scheme (NDIS) for Australia. The NDIS will help to cover the costs of support for people with significant and permanent disabilities. The NDIS commenced in mid 2013 in a limited number of launch sites in order to test the operation of the scheme and to allow for its design to be informed by feedback from people with a disability, their families and carers, service providers and community organisations.[1] As this monograph was written before the initial launch of NDIS, it contains no discussion of the launch sites or their evaluation.

The best available data suggests that the Indigenous population experiences profound or severe core activity limitations at more than double the rate of non-Indigenous Australians. These higher rates of disability mean that the NDIS is likely to be of significant benefit to Indigenous Australians.

Not only are rates of disability higher for Indigenous Australians, but many Indigenous people also face significant barriers to accessing disability planning and support services. In part this is due to the substantially higher proportion of the Indigenous population living in remote and very remote areas which generally lack disability services; services not always being responsive to or compatible with the cultural values of some Indigenous people; and Indigenous Australians disproportionately experiencing barriers associated with socioeconomic factors such as low income and low levels of literacy and numeracy.

Addressing these barriers—and indeed the whole question of addressing Indigenous disability —are further complicated by the fact that while across 'mainstream Australia' there has been a developing understanding of the notion of 'disability' and its impact on people's lives, there are a number of differences in the way in which Indigenous Australians view disability. The differences across Australia in how Indigenous Australians view disability complicate any attempt to address these barriers, and indeed to address Indigenous disability more generally. This reflects both questions of how Indigenous people and communities generally view disability and the extent to which they have been participants, or more frequently non-participants, in wider community change. That there is no simple conception or cultural view of disability is an important starting point, and one which is recognised in the preamble to the United Nations Convention on the Rights of Persons with Disabilities which

---

1   The launch sites are South Australia (for children 0–14 years), Tasmania (young people aged 15–24 years), Australian Capital Territory (all age groups), Barwon region of New South Wales (all age groups) and the Hunter region of New South Wales (all age groups).

notes 'that disability is an evolving concept' (United Nations (UN) 2006). Over recent years this evolution has been impacted by many factors, including the work of advocacy groups, events such as the 1981 International Year of Disabled Persons and the introduction of the *Disability Discrimination Act 1992*, as well as evolving community attitudes.

According to the First Peoples Disability Network (FPDN: 2011), many Indigenous people with disabilities do not identify as having a disability. This may be due in part to a reluctance to adopt additional labels of disadvantage, as well as a markedly different cultural perception of disability.

The terms of reference for the project upon which this monograph is based outline two distinct but related pieces of work. Accordingly, the first part of this monograph aims to identify and assess the range of disability service delivery models available in order to overcome the barriers to accessing disability support services experienced by Indigenous Australians. The second part analyses existing quantitative data sets to ascertain the extent and nature of disability in the Indigenous population, and how this varies according to geographic remoteness and key population groups. The work is intended to inform future policy development of a national scheme, and thereby assist Indigenous Australians in accessing support services appropriate to their cultural and geographic needs; sharing in opportunities available to the general Australian population; and participating fully in the economic and social life of their community.

This monograph is in three parts. Chapters 2–3 provide background and contextual information which is relevant to the disability service needs of the Indigenous population and how the NDIS can best meet the needs of Indigenous Australians. Chapter 4 considers the existing statistical evidence regarding the extent and nature of disability in the Indigenous population, the data gaps and how these gaps can best be filled. Chapters 5–8 focus on issues concerning the delivery of disability services to Indigenous Australians as part of the NDIS. Some possible models and approaches to service delivery are discussed and, drawing upon the available evidence base, the advantages and disadvantages of different models are outlined. The final chapter integrates the conclusions and offers recommendations.

Overview of the NDIS

In April 2008, the then Parliamentary Secretary for Disabilities and Children's Services, the Hon. Bill Shorten, established the Disability Investment Group (DIG). The Group's role was to explore innovative funding ideas from the private sector that would help people with disabilities and their families to access increased current support and life-long security. The possible model proposed by DIG was a National Disability Insurance Scheme (NDIS) that would fund individuals based on their needs, replacing the current system of capped programs and services. It was proposed that the scheme be funded from general revenue or a levy similar to the funding arrangements for Medicare. The first recommendation from DIG (2009: 6) was that 'the Commonwealth Government, in consultation with States and Territories, immediately commission a comprehensive feasibility study into a National Disability Insurance Scheme'.

In early 2010, the Productivity Commission was asked by the Australian Government to inquire into the feasibility and structure of a cost-effective 'National Disability Long-term Care and Support Scheme.' The Terms of Reference for the Productivity Commission inquiry ask that the Productivity Commission consider an approach that:

- provides long-term essential care and support for eligible people with a severe or profound disability, on an entitlement basis and taking into account the desired outcomes for each person over a lifetime

- is intended to cover people with disability not acquired as part of the natural process of ageing

- calculates and manages the costs of long-term care and support for people with severe and profound disability

- replaces the existing system of funding for the eligible population

- ensures a range of support options is available, including individualised approaches

- comprises a coordinated package of care services which could include accommodation support, aids and equipment, respite, transport, and a range of community participation and day programs available for a person's lifetime

- assists the person with disability to make decisions about their support

- offers support for people to participate in employment where possible.

The Productivity Commission (2011) identified four key issues with regards to the system of disability services operating in Australia at the time of its report.

- First, it argued that the disability system is significantly underfunded and that as a consequence individuals with a disability who are in need of a particular service or support (e.g. wheelchairs) are either unable to obtain the service they need or are subject to excessive waiting periods due to what is termed the rationing of services.

- Second, there is uncertainty in how services are allocated, which can make it very difficult for people with a disability or their carers to effect long-term planning decisions. Part of this uncertainty is due to a lack of integration across agencies and jurisdictions.

- Third, differences between States and Territories in the nature, timing and coverage of services provided mean that when individuals cross State/Territory borders the services they are entitled to receive may change.

- Fourth, people with a disability and their carers lack choice or control over the services they receive.

It is argued by the Productivity Commission that although a significant injection of funds would alleviate rationing and supply issues, the three factors of uncertainty, lack of consistency across States, and lack of choice would cause significant limitations to persist.

For this reason the Productivity Commission proposed a new NDIS which would not only substantially increase the level of funding for disability services, but would also combine the funding under a single, national framework. While this framework would be consistent across jurisdictions, the aim would be to provide much greater choice and control at the individual level. The scheme would be established alongside a new, no-fault National Injury Insurance Scheme, which would cover individuals who acquire a disability through catastrophic injury.

In the 2012–13 federal budget $1 billion was set aside for the development of the first stage of an NDIS. The NDIS launch took place in mid 2013, with services provided to around 10 000 people with significant and permanent disabilities in select locations across the country. There have been further developments for the NDIS since the work for this monograph was undertaken. Most importantly, the way in which the scheme is intended to operate in the NDIS launch sites is described in the draft National Disability Insurance Scheme (NDIS) Bill introduced into Parliament on Thursday 29 November 2012.

As noted above, the Terms of Reference for the report which forms the basis of this monograph were that the Productivity Commission-proposed design of the NDIS be used as the starting point. This necessitates the following summary of key aspects of the Productivity Commission's proposed design.

Key characteristics of the NDIS

Eligibility and assessment

The Productivity Commission proposal is for a system comprising three tiers of beneficiaries. The first tier of beneficiaries covers all Australians, including those without a disability or who are not carers. The NDIS is designed to provide reassurance for all Australians that in the event of themselves or someone they care for acquiring a significant or permanent disability they will be able to obtain assistance under the NDIS if they are not covered by another scheme such as workers compensation or motor vehicle accident compensation.

The second tier of beneficiaries are all those with a disability or who are carers, but who do not receive financial support under the NDIS. The Productivity Commission (2011: 15) estimates that this includes approximately 4 million Australians and, in addition, 800 000 carers. This second tier of recipients would receive information and referral services, and general information regarding the most effective care and support services for their particular needs.

The third tier of beneficiaries consists of people with significant care and support needs due to a permanent disability who would receive financial support from the NDIS. Permanent disabilities include episodic and chronic disabilities. Also covered would be those with significant and enduring psychiatric disability. This tier would not include people covered by other schemes, but may include those acquiring new catastrophic injuries who are covered by the National Injury Insurance Scheme; those with certain health conditions for which the publicly funded healthcare system is better suited; and a limited number acquiring a disability after commencement of the age pension.

The two main groups within the Tier 3 group are people with 'significantly reduced functioning in self-care, communication, mobility or self-management' who 'require significant ongoing support', and people who fall within an 'early intervention group' (Productivity Commission 2011: 14). It is estimated that the former comprises roughly 330 000 individuals, whereas the latter totals 80 000 people, for whom 'intervention would be safe, significantly improve outcomes and would be cost-effective.' It is also pointed out by the Productivity Commission that 'eligibility would be determined by functional limitations, not conditions'.

This focus on need as opposed to disabling conditions adds a significant degree of complexity to assessing eligibility. The proposed screening mechanism is that at the first stage when individuals approach the newly created agency responsible for the scheme they will be administered a short assessment module designed to identify whether they are likely to be eligible for a funded package. Those assessed as ineligible will then fall into Tier 2 of the scheme and, if necessary, be directed towards appropriate services not funded by the NDIS.

For those who are assessed as likely to be eligible a more detailed assessment process will then be triggered. As summarised (Productivity Commission 2011: 336), this includes the completion of a more detailed self-reported questionnaire; review by a trained assessor, including review of medical certificates; a meeting between this assessor and a local area coordinator; and a review and costing of the assessment by the National Disability Insurance Agency. While the assessment process is expected to be resource intensive, it is necessary in order to implement targeted and limited eligibility criteria.

This strict distinction between Tier 2 individuals—who receive minimal funding—and Tier 3 individuals—who receive an extensive range of support as documented below—places pressure on the operation of the assessment mechanism, a crucial aspect of the scheme.

Once assessed as being in Tier 3, a draft support package will be developed that is either accepted by the relevant person or their carer/family member, or sent for further review.

Type of support provided

The Productivity Commission Report (2011: Box 2: 23) proposes that the following types of support be provided to people with a significant and permanent disability who are covered by the NDIS.

- Aids and appliances, as well as home and vehicle modifications.

- Personal care that supports an individual to take care of themselves in their home and community.

- Community access supports. These are designed to provide opportunities for people to enjoy their full potential for social independence, and include facility and home-based activities, as well as supervision and physical care.

- Respite to provide a short-term and time-limited break for people with disabilities, families and other voluntary carers of people with a disability.

- Specialist accommodation support, such as group homes and alternative family placement.

- Domestic assistance to enable individuals to live in the community and live on their own, such as meal preparation and other domestic tasks; banking and shopping; assistance with selecting and planning activities, and attending appointments.

- Transport assistance to provide or coordinate individual or group transport services.

- Supported employment services and specialist transition to work programs that prepare people for jobs.

- Therapies such as occupational and physiotherapy, counselling, and specialist behavioural interventions.

- Local area coordination and development. These are broad services, including individual or family-focused case management and brokerage.

- Crisis/emergency support.

- Guide dogs and assistance dogs.

Methods of providing support

The Productivity Commission proposed two broad approaches to how the package of support is to be provided. The first is self-directed funding, where individuals or their carers 'cash out their individualised package of supports and manage their own budget' (Productivity Commission 2011: 346). The second is through choice of provider, where individuals are given an individualised package of support items, rather than a budget, with the ability to choose the service provider from whom the items will be sourced. There is also considerable scope in the proposed model for individuals to opt for self-directed funding for some types of services, but choice of provider for other aspects.

The self-directed funding model places a greater degree of risk onto the individual. However, this comes with the potential benefit of being able to make savings in one area which will lead to scope for additional expenditure in another area. There are likely to be differences in the extent to which people are able to realise the potential efficiency gains from a self-directed funding model. For example, individuals or carers with a high level of education are more likely to be able to negotiate or obtain low-cost services. People living in highly urbanised and more socioeconomically advantaged areas are likely to have a broad range of services available to them, and will therefore benefit from the self-directed funding model. The Productivity Commission Report notes that for those in regional—and to a lesser extent, remote—areas with practical, everyday needs, it will not be difficult to find the required services. However, this is less likely to be true for those with complex needs, a group into which Indigenous Australians disproportionately fall.

There are a number of eligibility restrictions for self-directed funding proposed by the Productivity Commission. Chief among these is an assessment that the individual is able to make the complex decisions required for such an approach. Where this is not possible, there is the option of guardians, including parents or partners, acting as the individual's agent. However, this not only places an additional burden on these carers—hence the voluntary nature of the self-directed funding—but also opens up the possibility of financial and other abuse. The Productivity Commission proposes a number of safeguards to mitigate these risks.

One of these safeguards or restrictions is that money from self-directed funding cannot be used to hire close family members. While it is important to minimise the risk that a close family member who is being paid to care for a person with a disability does not provide adequate care, the risk of this occurring needs to be weighed against the potential negative consequences of the restriction. In many regional and remote areas there may be few other available options than family members. Problems resulting from such a restriction are likely to be exacerbated in an Indigenous context in which kinship networks do not fit the standard western model of the nuclear family. The Productivity Commission Report (2011: 382) proposes a trial for employment of family members: if undertaken such a trial is likely to provide important data. However, it proposes a number of restrictions—including a decrease of the individual budget and a six-month limitation on paying family members—that may need to be reconsidered in regional and remote areas.

Recommendations of the Productivity Commission Report

The Productivity Commission Report identifies a number of issues related to Indigenous Australians that need to be considered in designing and implementing the NDIS. Specifically, Chapter 11 of the Productivity Commission Report focuses on the prevalence of disability within the Indigenous community, and how a future NDIS might address a number of other issues specific to Indigenous disability.

One of the issues identified by the Productivity Commission as requiring further consideration is whether in certain circumstances Indigenous people with a disability should be able to pay family members to provide disability support services. According to the Productivity Commission Report, the Australian Government spends 30 per cent more per capita on Indigenous Australians with disabilities than non-Indigenous Australians. However, considering the considerably higher costs of providing services in remote areas as well as the underreporting of Indigenous disability, it is likely that disadvantage in terms of access to services still exists.

A number of socioeconomic factors are relevant to the high rate of disability observed among Indigenous Australians, and a large gap in disability rates persists between Indigenous and non-Indigenous Australians. The Productivity Commission (2011) describes this relationship in which poor socioeconomic outcomes greatly increase rates of disability, which further compound socioeconomic disadvantage. Greater exposure to certain risk factors such as smoking and obesity contributed almost half of the difference in disability-adjusted years of life between Indigenous and non-Indigenous Australians (Productivity Commission 2011: 539).

Compounding these higher rates of disability are barriers that may prevent Indigenous Australians from accessing necessary disability services. Mistrust of—and lack of information about—government services is one of the primary barriers identified in the report. This mistrust might stem from negative past experiences, or simply from a feeling that government services are not applicable to a given individual's circumstances or cannot meet their needs. We will expand on these issues in a later section of this volume. However, the important point to note is that these cultural differences might be preventing some Indigenous Australians in seeking assistance from government service providers.

A further barrier to service use among Indigenous Australians with a disability is geographic; in 2006 around one-quarter of Indigenous Australians were living in remote or very remote areas, while only 1 per cent of non-Indigenous Australians did so. Geographical remoteness not only reduces the scope of services available to Indigenous communities, but also greatly increases the cost. Scarcity and proximity were found to be a bigger problem than cultural barriers, with half of Indigenous Australians seeking health services reporting having no available service in their area, and 45 per cent reporting distance and lack of transport as a barrier to accessing services (Productivity Commission 2011: 548).

A complicating factor is the age distribution of the Indigenous population. According to the Australian Bureau of Statistics (ABS) (2012a), 97 per cent of Indigenous Australians are aged 64 years and under, compared to 86 per cent of non-Indigenous Australians. This means that if the threshold was applied universally, Indigenous Australians would be more reliant on the NDIS as opposed to the aged care system. However, in Recommendation 3.6 of Productivity Commission (2011: 200) it is stated that 'a younger age threshold than the Age Pension age should apply to Indigenous people given their lower life expectancy, as is recognised under existing aged care arrangements'. However, this creates equity issues if the NDIS provides a higher level of support than the aged care system. It is important, therefore, that Indigenous Australians under the age of 65 be allowed to opt in or opt out of the NDIS (as opposed to the aged care system) based on their individual circumstances and assessment of needs.

The Productivity Commission Report recommends a lower level of NDIS funding for those aged less than 15 years compared to those aged 15 years or over. The recommendation for the lower level of funding for children is based on the assumption that 'that families provide most care to children between the ages of 0–14 years, regardless of disability, and that care should be provided predominantly to support parents in their role of caring for a child with a disability' and also on the assumption that the education system is responsible for providing some supports to children with a disability (Productivity Commission 2011: 767) and/or the child's family. However, this assumption may be problematic in an Indigenous context in which: (a) many Indigenous Australians do not participate as intensively in formal schooling, in part because of their disabilities; (b) many regional and remote schools may not be able to provide the same degree of support to students with a disability as can be provided by larger urban schools and an associated network of special schools; (c) the level of income and wealth of the households in which Indigenous Australians live is substantially lower; and (d) Indigenous children are more likely to be cared for by non-family members. The validity of the assumptions about the need for NDIS funding for children for the Indigenous population is particularly important given that 36 per cent of the Indigenous population is aged less than 15 years compared to 18 per cent of the non-Indigenous population.

While the NDIS for the most part will be based on a self-directed funding model, the feasibility of this in rural and remote communities is something that cannot be assumed. In some cases it is possible that a different approach is likely to be needed in these locations, with this having particular implications for providing disability services for Indigenous Australians who disproportionately live in these locations. Block-funding services constitute one way to overcome the problem of incomplete markets for disability services in remote communities. The Productivity Commission (2011) proposes a number of forms that this block-funding could take, including funding new or existing community organisations to provide services. Where such organisations are lacking, however, it might be necessary to fund larger organisations to provide managerial oversight and mentoring to build capacity over the longer term.

In order to ensure services are meeting the needs of Indigenous communities, the Productivity Commission (2011) proposes a number of strategies, including embedding these services within the community, employing Indigenous staff, and providing cultural awareness training to staff. The strategies clearly pose challenges of their own, including lack of existing expertise within the community, the difficulty of recruiting Indigenous staff, and the reservations individuals might have in accepting care from outsiders when this is necessary. These problems can be mitigated by adequate language and cultural awareness training, and by allowing for increased flexibility in working conditions in order to attract Indigenous employees.

The demographic and geographic context

This section summarises key demographic and geographic features of the Indigenous population that are of particular relevance to the design and implementation of the NDIS.

Indigenous age structure and projected growth of the Indigenous population

According to the preliminary 2011 Census population estimates, the median age of the Indigenous population is about 21 years for males and about 23 years for females. This is compared to 37 years and 39 years for non-Indigenous males and females respectively. The Indigenous population has a much younger age structure than that of the non-Indigenous population, as demonstrated in Fig. 1.1, which overlays the age distribution of the Indigenous and non-Indigenous populations, according to the percentage present in each age group. In comparing the two populations, it is clear that a much higher proportion of the Indigenous population is aged 24 years or less. Across males and females, these age groups represent 56 per cent of the total Indigenous population, compared to 32 per cent of the total non-Indigenous population. At the other end of the age distribution, 14 per cent of the total non-Indigenous population is aged 65 years and over, compared to 3 per cent of the Indigenous population.

The Indigenous population has been increasing at a faster rate than the non-Indigenous population. The preliminary population estimate for the Indigenous population in 2011 (ABS 2012a) was 30 per cent higher than the 2006 population estimate. By comparison, the non-Indigenous population estimate grew by only 7.3 per cent over the period. There are two main reasons why the Indigenous population has and will continue to grow at a faster rate than the non-Indigenous population. First, Indigenous women have a higher fertility rate than their non-Indigenous counterparts, with an Indigenous female expected to have 2.7 children over her reproductive life compared to the total female population expected to have 1.9 children (ABS 2012b). The second reason for higher growth rates is that, in addition to those children born to an Indigenous mother, a substantial number of Indigenous children have non-Indigenous mothers and Indigenous fathers. Nationally, 31 per cent of Indigenous children born in 2011 had two Indigenous parents and a further 42 per cent had an Indigenous mother and a non-Indigenous father. These births will have been captured by the Indigenous fertility rate mentioned in the previous paragraph. However, a further 27 per cent of Indigenous children had a non-Indigenous mother and an Indigenous father. These births represent an additional contribution to the Indigenous population.

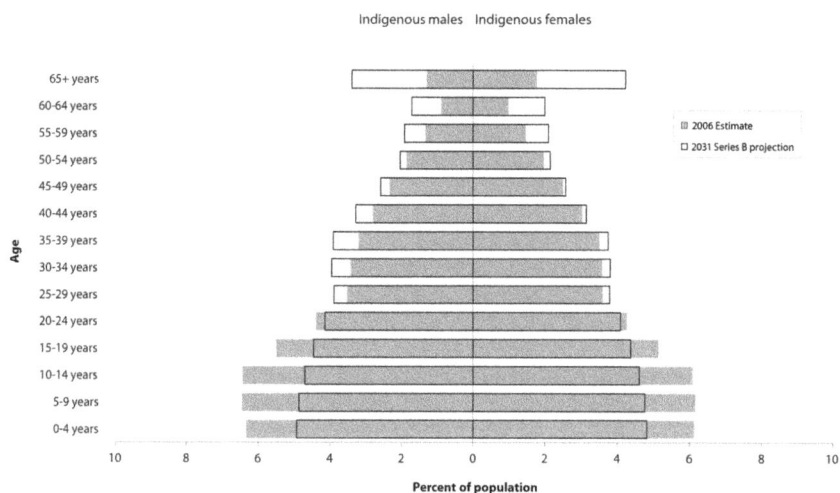

Fig. 1.1 Age distribution of the Indigenous and non-Indigenous population, Australia, 2011

Source: ABS 2012a

While it is clear that the Indigenous population will grow at a faster rate than the non-Indigenous population, it is very difficult to predict this growth accurately. For example, in using the 2006 Census, Biddle and Taylor (2009) projected that the Indigenous population would grow from just over 517 000 in 2006 to 848 000 in 2031 and that this trajectory would result in the Indigenous population being around 575 000 in 2011. However, the preliminary 2011 estimate (ABS 2012a) is that in 2011 the Indigenous population was around 670 000, approximately 17 per cent higher than the projections of Biddle and Taylor (2009). Although the current Indigenous population is relatively young, in part due to increasing longevity, it is likely that it will age noticeably in the future. While there is still a large gap in life expectancy between Indigenous and non-Indigenous Australians, age-specific mortality rates of the Indigenous population appear to be falling.

The projected age distribution of the Indigenous population in 2006 and 2031 indicated in Fig. 1.2, assumes convergence between Indigenous and non-Indigenous fertility and mortality rates over the period. The proportion of the Indigenous population aged 0–24 years is projected to fall from 57 per cent in 2006 to 46 per cent in 2031. Correspondingly, the proportion of the population aged 50 years and over is projected to increase from 12 per cent to 20 per cent between 2006 and 2031.

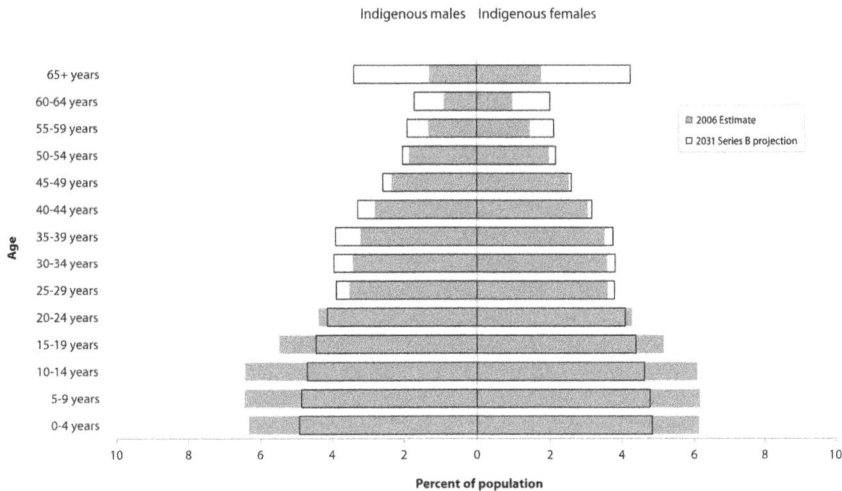

Fig. 1.2 Indigenous age distribution, Australia, 2006 (estimates) and 2031 (projections)

Source: Biddle and Taylor 2009

While we do not yet have official projections based on the 2011 Census, it should be noted that the fastest rate of growth in the Indigenous population between 2006 and 2011 was among those aged 50 years and over. Specifically, in comparison with 2006 estimates there were 47.6 per cent more Indigenous Australians aged 50 years and over in 2011. The projected increase in the number of Indigenous people aged 50–64 years, the upper end of the age distribution covered by the NDIS, combined with increasing rate of disability with age (see Chapter 2 of this volume) means that the number of Indigenous Australians within scope of the scheme will increase in coming decades.

The geographic distribution of the Indigenous population

While the majority of the Indigenous population lives in major cities (32%), inner regional (21%) and outer regional (22%) areas, a substantial proportion live in remote (10%) and very remote areas (16%). Overall, Indigenous Australians are much more likely to live in remote parts of the country relative to the non-Indigenous population. For example, while in 2006 (the most recent year for which we have remoteness estimates) 2.5 per cent of the total Australian population was estimated to be Indigenous, in major cities 1.2 per cent of the population are Indigenous. In remote areas 15 per cent of the population are Indigenous and in very remote areas 47.5 per cent of the population are Indigenous.

Using a region-based geography, Fig. 1.3 shows the proportion of the total Indigenous population estimated to live in each Indigenous Region (IREG) in 2011.[2] The differences between IREGs can be highlighted by comparing the remote 'region' of Apatula in central Australia with the city of Sydney. Apatula has an area of around 548 000 square kilometres and, in 2011, a total estimated population of 10 174 of whom 81 per cent were Indigenous, the highest percentage outside of the Torres Strait IREG. The Sydney-Wollongong IREG has an area of around 11 500 square kilometres and an estimated population in 2011 of 4 555 865, of whom just 1.1 per cent were Indigenous. Clearly, Apatula is much more Indigenous in its population makeup than Sydney. However, at the time of the 2011 Census, there were estimated to be 6.2 times as many Indigenous Australians living in Sydney as there were in Apatula. Indeed, 29 per cent of the total Indigenous population was estimated to live on the eastern seaboard between Sydney and Brisbane. This is 2.8 times as many as the whole of the Northern Territory (10% of the Indigenous population) and more than the combined Indigenous populations of Western Australia, South Australia and Tasmania.

What the results summarised in Fig. 1.3 make clear is that, even if rates of Indigenous disability were much lower in major cities and regional centres compared to remote parts of the country, the sheer weight of population means that the majority of the disability services provided to the Indigenous population as part of the NDIS will need to be provided in urban centres. On the other hand, however, most of the disability services in remote parts of the country will be used by Indigenous Australians. This geographic distribution also has clear service delivery and workforce implications, as discussed in Chapter 7.

---

2   Official Indigenous Region population estimates will not be available until late 2013. The results in Fig. 1.3 apply the state-specific undercount (from ABS 2012a) to Indigenous Region-specific census counts.

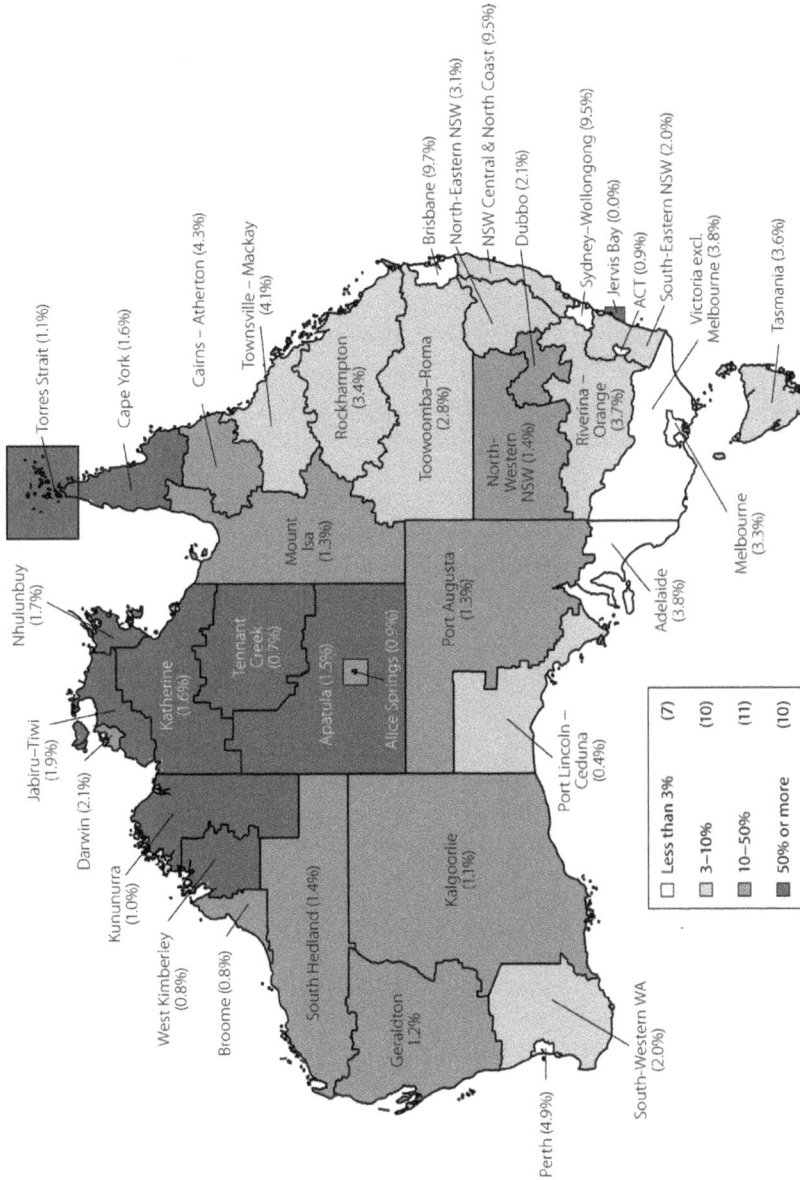

Fig. 1.3 Geographic distribution of the Indigenous population, Australia, 2011

Source: Customised calculations using ABS 2012a

It is anticipated that the Indigenous population will become more urbanised over the next few decades. This is driven by two factors. First, there has been a steady out-migration of the Indigenous population from remote areas to regional centres and major cities that shows no sign of abating in the future (Biddle 2009). Secondly, while Indigenous female fertility rates tend to be evenly spread across the country, most of the births of Indigenous children to non-Indigenous mothers occur in urban parts of the country. This is mainly due to the relatively high rates of intermarriage in these areas (Heard, Birrell and Khoo 2009).

Using data from the 2006 Census, Biddle and Taylor (2009) estimate that the Indigenous population in major cities will grow by 34 per cent between 2006 and 2016, compared to 9 per cent in very remote areas. While it is projected that the Indigenous population will increase in remote and very remote areas at a slower rate than in major cities and regional areas, the non-Indigenous population is projected to decline in remote and very remote Australia over the period 2006–2016, meaning that the proportion of the Indigenous population in these parts of the country will be higher in 2016 than it was in 2006. Early results from the 2011 Census suggest that, if anything, these trends are intensifying. A feature of the Indigenous population in remote and very remote areas is that it is spread throughout a very large number of small, discrete, largely Indigenous communities. This means that the absolute number of people in most discrete Indigenous communities that will be covered by the NDIS is quite low.

Analysis of the ABS Housing and Infrastructure in Aboriginal and Torres Strait Islander Communities Survey 2006 by the Australian National Audit Office (ANAO 2012) provides useful information on the number of discreet Indigenous communities, the population in these communities, and the average population of the communities according to geographic remoteness. Overall, 20 per cent of the 2006 Indigenous population lived in these identifiable discrete communities, mostly in non-urban locations, as shown in Table 1.1.

Table 1.1 Number of discrete Indigenous communities and population by remoteness area, Australia, 2006

Remoteness category	Number of communities	Population	Average population
Major city	4	346	87
Inner regional	19	1 870	98
Outer regional	52	10 254	197
Remote	104	11 237	108
Communities of less than 50	71	1 436	20
Communities of more than 50	33	9 801	297
Very remote	1 008	69 253	69
Communities of less than 50	767	8 723	11
Communities of more than 50	241	60 530	251
Total	1 187	92 960	78

Source: Derived from ANAO 2012: Table 1.3

The data shown in Table 1.1 highlights the large number of small Indigenous communities which exist in remote and very remote Australia. There were 1 187 discrete Indigenous communities in 2006 in which 92 960 Indigenous people were counted (20% of the Indigenous population). The average population of these communities was 78. The vast majority of the discrete communities are in very remote areas (1 008), with an additional 104 such communities in remote areas. Of the 1 008 discrete communities in very remote areas, 767 have less than 50 people living in them, and 241 have a population of 50 or more. The communities in very remote areas with a population of less than 50 people, have a total population of 8 723 and an average population of just 11. The communities with a population of greater than 50 have a total population of 60 530 and an average population of 251.

Indigenous notions of and approaches to disability

Disability, health and community participation

As with non-Indigenous Australians, the lived experience of Indigenous people with disabilities is complex and personal. Further, as discussed previously, the cultural concept of disability is one that continues to evolve. This complexity is further nuanced by the diversity of cultures and traditions among Indigenous Australian communities. However, there are particular cultural and historical factors that play an important role in how Indigenous Australians approach disability as a concept, and how it is experienced by the individual and by the community.

It has often been observed that there is no word for disability in many Indigenous languages. Ariotti (1999: 218) notes that the Pitjantjatjara language has no single word that captures the idea of disability; instead, specific words are used for particular ailments, such as *kuru pati* (blind), *pina pati* (deaf), *witapitjara* (to have back pain) or *lurpani* (to hobble around). The lack of an abstract concept of disability goes beyond language, as found by King (2010) in her interviews with Indigenous users of a respite centre in Brisbane. Despite being regular users of disability services, and requiring assistance with a range of day-to-day tasks, the women she interviewed simply did not identify themselves or the people around them as having a disability. When asked if they could remember people from their communities with a disability, few could recall any such individuals. Furthermore, even when disability is recognised, it is mostly not considered a salient issue when compared with problems such as unemployment, poverty, discrimination and chronic disease. A further factor is that the higher rate of disability in the Indigenous population may 'normalise' perceptions of disability.

In order to understand how disability is conceptualised by Indigenous Australians today, it is important to understand both the history of disability in Indigenous Australia, and more generally the history of Indigenous people in their interface with other elements of Australian society and in particular their relationship with government and welfare services, including the extent to which the Indigenous community has had voice in the wider conceptualisation of disability within Australian society. One attempt to do this has been by Ariotti (1999) who describes three broad phases in this history: impairment, oppression, and empowerment. In the impairment phase, '[d]isability did not exist' (Ariotti 1999: 217). This is not to say that no members of the Indigenous population had physical or mental impairments; rather, there was no concept of disability that separated those individuals from the rest of their community. In the oppression phase, the concept of disability was first constructed for Indigenous Australians by non-Indigenous Australians; the introduction of this concept had cognitive, behavioural and social impacts for Indigenous Australians. As well adapting to the new concept of disability, its introduction also had behavioural consequences. Unlike the impairment phase, in which individuals are treated no differently by the group, the labelling of a person as having a disability has the potential to separate them from their community. This may lead to an individual's internalisation of helplessness, and the realisation that they require assistance and are thus potentially a burden. Labelling an individual as having a disability might not only cause shame but also may threaten their place in the community, with many Indigenous Australians having experienced family members being removed because of physical or mental impairment. Ariotti's final stage, the empowerment stage, reflects recent desires within the Indigenous community to reconstruct the idea of disability in a way that is culturally appropriate, a goal that is reflected in the work of organisations like the FPDN.

While there is very little research into how contemporary groups of Indigenous people view the concept of disability, the limited evidence that is available suggests that Indigenous Australians are less likely to identify as having a disability compared to non-Indigenous people with a similar level of impairment and that, where it is used, the concept of disability is more closely linked to notions of community participation and belonging (King 2010). While there are a range of views and experiences within the Indigenous population, the connection between disability, health and community participation suggests that for the Indigenous population assisting individuals with a disability to participate as fully as possible in community life is likely to be particularly important. The FPDN (2011: 14) criticises many disability services for ignoring the importance of participation, suggesting that the services are '...dealing only with the health aspects through the provision of a technical aid without addressing the systemic barriers that impact the person's life, such as an inaccessible community'.

If a disability makes it hard for a person to travel then it is likely that Indigenous Australians with a disability will not be able to participate fully in expected cultural activities (e.g. funerals). While this is an issue in both remote and non-remote areas, it is likely be a bigger issue in remote areas where, for example, an individual's disability might prevent them from travelling by light plane if it is not properly fitted for wheelchairs. Furthermore, the individual might require special care that is not available when visiting other communities (Senior 2000: 8). As well as the inability to travel long distances, a disability might prevent an individual from participating in cultural activities closer to home, such as going into the bush to fish or camp (Senior 2000: 20). Accessible transport was one of the key issues identified in the FPDN submission to the Productivity Commission Inquiry into Disability Care and Support.

The care of Indigenous people with a disability

A unifying theme in much of the research into disability in the Indigenous community is the importance of caring for people with impairments within the family and wider community. Senior (2000) reports that within Indigenous society, responsibility for caring for those with disabilities as well as the elderly traditionally rests with the immediate and extended family. Senior (2000: 19) notes that '[i]t was commonly stated that it was families' responsibility to look after people with disabilities, and that caring for people and helping one another was a very important part of life and also as how people viewed themselves'.

The experience of Indigenous Australians with disabilities is thus highly dependent on the ability of their family members to provide the necessary care. While this might not pose a problem for individuals with straightforward needs, many individuals with disabilities have complex requirements, often compounded by the co-prevalence of multiple diseases or disabilities.

The ability to care for family members with disabilities is further complicated when families must care for multiple individuals, experience poverty or where family breakdown occurs. The high incidence of chronic disease and poverty related problems in Indigenous communities makes it more likely that families will struggle with caring for individuals with a disability, especially when the carers often suffer health problems of their own. This magnified burden of care has been identified by health workers, carers and people with disabilities as a serious issue in Indigenous communities (Senior 2000: 22).

While the family is traditionally the primary source of care for Indigenous people with disabilities, the extended kinship group and wider community also plays an important role in providing care and assistance. This care can take a range of forms, from informal assistance provided by one person to another, to more formal arrangements in which the community arranges professional care for an individual. Ariotti (1999: 221) describes the role of the Ngaanyatjarra Pitjantjatjara Yankunytjatjara Women's Council, which has introduced an employment service and mental health program, as well as employing a physiotherapist, two traditional healers, and a social worker.

Demand for disability services

Barriers to increased use of disability services by Indigenous Australians can generally be considered in terms of supply side and demand side issues. The supply side will be discussed in detail in a later section of this volume. While not always framed in these terms, on the demand side the perceptions of disability discussed above are often cited as the reason disability services are underused in Indigenous communities (e.g. FPDN 2011). One potential problem identified in the literature is that of the shame felt by individuals who believe they are a burden on their community, and also by carers who feel that they cannot provide adequate assistance (King 2010: 196).

Lack of knowledge about access to services is a related issue, as shame may prevent Indigenous Australians from seeking out information concerning services available to them. Senior identifies reluctance among many Indigenous Australians with disabilities to seek assistance when issues of disability and poor health are often seen as something out of their control (Senior 2000: 22). Another common reason given for the limited use of services is negative past experiences with government services, notably where these involve outsiders entering an individual's home. The concern was often raised that care workers who came into an Indigenous person's home, for respite care for example, would be disparaging of the person regarding the cleanliness of their home (King 2010: 205). Further to these barriers are issues surrounding the cultural appropriateness of disability services being offered, including the gender and cultural background of carers.

Frameworks for disability and other service delivery models

The Productivity Commission Report (2011) proposes a move towards a model of service delivery that places much greater focus on choice and competition.

This model should be seen in the context of increasing reliance on such approaches across a range of social and community services. To provide an overview of the advantages and disadvantages of different models for delivering government services, we turn to *The Other Invisible Hand* by Le Grand (2007). According to Le Grand, services can be delivered under four different models: trust, targets and performance management, voice, and choice and competition.

Trust

According to Le Grand (2007: 16), under the trust model, 'government sets the overall budget for the service; those who provide the service spend it as they wish.' The underlying assumption of this model is that the public servants who are providing the service (e.g. doctors, nurses, teachers, social workers) do so under mainly altruistic motivations. Any interference by government in terms of how services are to be allocated will be inefficient, either because it does not have the level of expertise or local insight that professionals possess, or because doing so will lead to an erosion of the intrinsic motivation held by the professionals.

The main benefit of this model, therefore, is that the knowledge of public service professionals working in a complex environment has the potential of being implemented in the most efficient and effective way possible. A potential limitation of the trust model, however, is that the incentives of service providers in the public service do not always overlap with the best interests of either the patient or the system. Where there is a conflict in such incentives there is a strong possibility that resources will be allocated inefficiently.

Targets and performance management

In many ways the opposite to trust, the system of targets and performance management assumes that service providers are motivated less by public (or patient/student/client) interest and more by their self-interest. Variously labelled command-and-control, or mistrust, 'workers are instructed or in other ways directed to deliver a good service by a higher authority' (Le Grand 2007: 1). This direction generally takes the form of numerical targets. Meeting or exceeding these targets will result in rewards, including financial bonuses or greater autonomy for staff and/or the organisation. Failure to meet targets, on the other hand, results in various penalties including greater outside intervention, demotion or dismissal of senior staff, or public censure.

The obvious benefit of a system of targets is that it does not rely on the altruism of professionals in the system. In addition, it allows decisions to be made by a central authority that is able to shape priorities for the system as a whole. However, this central authority is unlikely to be aware of mitigating factors at the local level. Furthermore, if workers are motivated by their self-interest, they are as likely to favour decisions benefiting themselves regardless of systemic disadvantage as they are to work with it, and are less likely to seek continuous improvement once threshold targets have been set. Using targets as a means to allocate resources can lead to serious negative consequences for motivation and morale, especially among those workers who are used to a high degree of autonomy.

In addition the practical design of targets and performance management systems often present some difficulties. These systems frequently face a conflict between simple outcome measurement designed to focus the system on the desired goals, and the extent to which specifying these targets can be difficult and the system is open to abuse through processes such as 'creaming', or, where the targets are of necessity only an approximation of the outcome sought, the extent to which providers will seek to achieve the target, rather than the broader outcome it is meant to represent.

Voice

A limitation of both trust and targets as a system of delivering services is that the priorities within the system are set by service providers (in the case of the former) or funding agencies (in the case of the latter). The only way in which the interests of users of the service are taken into account is indirectly, through the ballot box, or on an ad hoc basis, through informal discussions with service providers. An alternative way to allocate services is by providing a direct avenue for users to shape the priorities within the system. One way to do this is through voice, a catch-all description by which 'users of public services communicate their views directly to service providers' (Le Grand 2007: 1). This can be done individually or collectively.

Collective voice mechanisms have the benefit of conveying the needs and interests of the community at the local level. This can provide very useful information to service providers. However, in order for systems of voice to exert a beneficial effect on the quality of service provision, those providing the service need to be sufficiently motivated to act in the user's interest, as opposed to their own. Another limitation of using such mechanisms to allocate services is that not everyone within the community has the same capacity for their voice to be heard. Those who are relatively disadvantaged based on their age, sex, income, geography or ethnicity are less likely to have their interests taken into account than dominant groups within the society.

Choice and competition

The final system for allocating services discussed in Le Grand (2007), and the one which occupies the majority of the discussion, is choice and competition. Here, 'users choose the service they want from those offered by competing providers' (Le Grand 2007: 1). In this system, choice can manifest in a number of ways, including 'choice of provider (where)…choice of professional (who)… choice of service (what)…choice of time (when)…[and] choice of access channel or method of communication (how)' (Le Grand 2007: 39–40). On the supply side, competition is the 'presence in the public service of a number of providers, each of which, for one reason or another, are motivated to attract users of the particular service' (Le Grand 2007: 41).

There are four main arguments for a system of choice and competition as a model for public service delivery. First, by providing a greater level of autonomy to service users, choice can be seen as a beneficial outcome in and of itself. Second, it can encourage providers to be more responsive to user needs, thereby leading to services which are of greater quality. This higher quality can be achieved regardless of whether the service providers are completely altruistic or completely self-interested. The former, it is argued, are likely to provide a better service because they are motivated by maximising client satisfaction. The latter provide a better service because it is in their economic interest to do so. Third, choice and competition can lead to services being delivered more efficiently by creating incentives for providers to offer the same level of services at a lower cost.

The final benefit of choice and competition, its proponents claim, is that services are provided more equitably by reducing the opportunity for those with greater political clout to demand preferable service. However, this comes at the cost of providing scope for those with greater financial resources to obtain a superior service. This can be mitigated to a certain extent by the use of quasi-markets in which individuals do not use their own resources to purchase goods and services, but rather use money provided by the government in the form of a voucher or a specially formulated budget. Equity criteria are still not met, however, unless individuals are restricted from purchasing additional services.

In order for a choice and competition model to result in the above benefits, three criteria need to be met—'competition must be real; users must be properly informed, especially ones who are less well off; and opportunities and incentives for selection or cream-skimming must be eliminated' (Le Grand 2007: 76–7). The latter refers to the situation where providers maximise profits by excluding those clients who are more difficult to service and are hence more costly. Examples of this include private schools which receive government funds excluding students with learning or behavioural difficulties, or health providers excluding those patients with more serious conditions and/or multiple conditions. The potential for cream-skimming can be minimised by removing the ability of service providers to choose the clients that they administer to, or by adding a disadvantage premium, whereby the service providers receive additional payments for those clients deemed to be disadvantaged.

A further limitation of the choice and competition model is the necessity for a large number of users to ensure a well-functioning market. This is unlikely to be met for relatively rare conditions or, more generally, in rural and remote parts of a country. In these circumstances, governments will be required to underwrite a certain level of services. Le Grand (2007) argues that this problem can be mitigated to an extent by franchising— a system whereby a local monopoly service is offered to a single provider under a fixed-term contract that is renewed on a competitive semi-regular basis. However, even then, in a country like Australia (as opposed to the United Kingdom) there are likely to be many areas where that option is not profitable for service providers.

Direct payments and disability service provision

While there are a number of examples where direct payments for social services have been used in Australia, such a framework is much more widespread and has a longer history in the United Kingdom. Glasby and Littlechild (2009) examine the recent changes to the British social care system, including the expansion of direct payments and the introduction of personal budgets as means of financing community care. Glasby and Littlechild (2009) describe the evolution of the British social care system from one based on a paternalistic Professional Gift philosophy (where support is defined and controlled by professionals and given as a unilateral gift to the needy), to one based on the principles of independent living. After the Second World War the *1948 National Assistance Act* distinguished between the financial and non-financial welfare needs of social service users, allocating responsibility for these two separate bodies. The authors argue that this purely artificial distinction could not meet the complex needs of service users, and restricted the scope of social work in the period after the war. The emphasis during this period was on directly providing services which, echoing the discussion in Le Grand (2007), has been criticised as inflexible, unreliable, and giving the service user little control or choice in the kind of assistance they require.

In response to these criticisms and the growing strength of the Independent Living Movement, the Independent Living Fund was introduced in 1988, introducing direct payments as an option for local authorities in funding social care. Applications for the Independent Living Fund were not expected to number more than around 300 per year, but by 1993, 22 000 people were receiving payments though the fund (Glasby and Littlechild 2009: 14). Its popularity, according to Glasby and Littlechild (2009), was due to the freedom it gave in choice of service provider, increased continuous care without disruption, flexibility and a greater breadth of care arrangements, but most importantly the feeling of self-respect that many of the fund's users reported. Due to financial limitations, eligibility for the Independent Living Fund was progressively tightened, and eventually the fund was discontinued in anticipation of replacement by a new system.

As the Independent Living Fund was wound back, local authorities were still able to make indirect payments, whether to third parties or trusts, in order to fund social care, and in 1994 just under 60 per cent of authorities surveyed reported doing so (Glasby and Littlechild 2009: 27). Legal issues surrounding these indirect payments, as well as increasing vocal lobbying from disability advocacy groups, finally lead to the 1996 *Community Care (Direct Payments) Act*, which gave authorities the power (but not the duty) to provide direct payments for community care services. Direct payments were only to be authorised if it could be shown that the service user was both willing to receive the payments and able to manage them. Furthermore, authorities were directed to make direct payments only if they were more cost effective than providing the services directly.

Because of the voluntary nature of this system, as well as the guidelines described above, it is unsurprising that uptake of direct payments has been uneven across the country and between different user groups. In 2006–07 only 3.2 per cent of adults receiving community based services were recipients of direct payments (Glasby and Littlechild 2009: 42). The authors identify a number of factors that appear to impact the uptake of this scheme: local concerns about the privatisation of social care, the flexibility of existing purchasing arrangements, and the influence of the disability movement. This last factor was found to be especially significant, with a high correlation recorded between the uptake of direct payments and the prevalence of user-led advocacy and support schemes in a given area.

In the 2006 National Centre for Independent Living report on direct payments discussed in Glasby and Littlechild (2009), the conditions most conducive to increased uptake of direct payments are summarised as follows: sufficient levels of support provided to users; good knowledge of direct payments among local authorities and community/voluntary groups; local authorities taking a strategic lead on direct payments; users who are involved in all areas of the payments; and a sound understanding of the principles of independent living (Glasby and Littlechild 2009: 38).

A further evolution of direct payments, namely personal budgets, were first introduced in 2003 on a small scale, allowing individuals even more input into how they allocated their resources, with guidance from social workers as needed. The authors describe personal budgets as an important progression from direct payments in terms of the principles of Independent Living. Under the direct payment scheme, users were still constrained to purchasing certain services and were allocated fixed sums with which to do so. Personal budgets, on the other hand, allow flexibility and creativity in how users decide to meet their needs, which the authors argue leads to efficiency gains as well as an increased sense of independence and control.

Preliminary findings from pilot programs suggest that personal budgets have led to important welfare improvements for the majority of users, as well as cost savings of around 10 per cent, and in some instances significantly greater savings (Glasby and Littlechild 2009: 92). One group for which personal budgets did not appear to have such a positive result was elderly service users, who might have found managing their own support a burden compared with other groups.

The authors argue that both the direct payment scheme and the small number of personal budget programs have had a significant impact on the wellbeing of service users, and contribute greatly to the goal of independent living. Direct payment recipients are found to be happier than direct service recipients, citing choice and control as the two most important factors in their wellbeing (Glasby and Littlechild 2009: 113). One of the most important aspects of the direct payment system identified by the authors was the ability of service users to take their custom elsewhere when not satisfied with the service provided—that is, 'empowerment by exit' (Glasby and Littlechild 2009: 133). Improved mental and physical health have also been attributed to direct payments, as users are able to tailor services to their personal needs, thus increasing the effectiveness of the services (Glasby and Littlechild 2009: 118). Furthermore, the authors argue that direct payments and personal budgets have the potential to result in significant cost savings due to increased efficiency, thus alleviating the burden on public spending.

Like Le Grand (2007), however, Glasby and Littlechild (2009) identify a number of barriers to the successful expansion of both the direct payment and personal budget programs. First, for empowerment by exit to be a realistic goal of these systems, acceptable alternatives have to exist, information about these alternatives must be available, and switching service providers must be easy (Glasby and Littlechild 2009: 133). This might not be possible in rural areas, especially in terms of recruiting personal assistance staff. While employing close relatives is not permitted under the direct payment system in the United Kingdom, the authors argue that this rule might need to be relaxed in order to overcome the problem of recruitment in rural areas.

Minority ethnic groups are also likely to face additional barriers in accessing direct payments if assessment processes do not adequately take into account cultural background and requirements in terms of care, especially if there is a lack of advocacy or support services. This is not guaranteed, though; Glasby and Littlechild (2009: 154) cite the example of one region in which minority ethnic groups comprised 20 per cent of the population but only 1 per cent of those accessing traditional social services. However, after the introduction of personal budgets, this proportion had risen to 10 per cent. Another potential barrier the authors foresee in the expansion of the direct payments system is financial; the very cost effective nature of this system might lead to less resources being devoted to community care overall if governments perceive direct payments as a cost cutting mechanism.

The authors identify a number of risks that must be addressed if direct payments and personal budgets are to become the norm in social care. Some commentators have expressed concern that direct budgets will lead to a two-tier system of social care, in which wealthier, educated individuals gain access to better services. The authors disagree with this assessment, arguing that, if anything, direct payments will place service users on a more equal footing, as they will be less subject to the inbuilt inequalities of the current care system. Another risk identified is that of exploitation of social carers, most notably underpayment, being forced to work antisocial hours, or not possessing paid insurance. The authors agree that direct payments are likely to result in more cash-in-hand work, and that this can lead to the above problems, but that this issue is not unique to the social care sector. Child benefits paid to parents are often spent on unofficial work such as babysitting and cleaning, they argue; direct payments to individuals with a disability should not be seen as a new problem. Furthermore, they argue that these issues are to some extent due to financial restrictions, and that social care users often express a desire to pay higher wages, including insurance and holiday pay to their personal assistants, if their payments were more generous. Despite these issues, the authors report that 95 per cent of personal assistants who were employed using direct payments were satisfied with their role (Glasby and Littlechild 2009: 150).

The authors also discuss potential risks to the service users themselves, notably from rogue operators who have not acquired sufficient experience in social care, or who potentially pose a threat to the user. The authors see a role for the government in regulating the sector to mitigate these risks, including training and inspections, but they stress that ultimately people with a disability should accept the same risks as everyone else with regards to hiring personal assistants. The authors suggest that these risks can be managed by putting in place adequate support for service users, including peer support networks. Overall, the authors believe that these risks are manageable, and should not prevent the successful uptake of direct payments and personal budgets for more social care users.

2. Disability in the Indigenous population

It is well established that the prevalence of disability among Indigenous Australians is significantly higher than that of the general population (AIHW 2009a). Indigenous Australians are at greater risk of disability, in part because they are more frequently subject to predictive factors including low birth weight, chronic disease and infectious diseases (e.g. ear infections such as otitis media, especially in young children). In addition, the Indigenous population has an increased risk of acquiring disability through accidents and violence, mental health problems and substance abuse. There is greater prevalence of these factors in communities where there are higher rates of unemployment, lower levels of income, poorer diet and living conditions, and poorer access to adequate health care, early intervention and rehabilitation services. Indigenous people with a disability are also significantly over-represented among homeless people, in the criminal and juvenile justice systems, and in the care and protection system, both as parents and children.

Not only are rates of disability higher for Indigenous Australians than for other Australians, they also face significant additional barriers to accessing disability planning and support services. In part this is due to a lack of disability services and disability-friendly housing and transport in remote areas. However, even in non-remote areas there are barriers to access related to services not always being responsive to Indigenous cultural values.

This chapter explores the nature and extent of disability among the Indigenous population, including analyses by age, remoteness and State/Territory. Where relevant, comparisons with the non-Indigenous population and to Indigenous persons without disability are provided. Data on the use of disability support services by Indigenous Australians and the barriers faced in accessing services is provided. The final section assesses the strengths and gaps in available data sources and offers recommendations to fill these gaps in order to inform future data collection and analyses in this area.

Measuring disability

A disability may be an impairment of body structure or function, a limitation in activities, and/or a restriction in participation of a person in specific activities. A person's functioning or disability is conceived as an interaction between health conditions and environmental and personal factors. The International

Classification of Functioning, Disability and Health (ICF) describes functioning and disability in terms of three key components: body functions and structures, activities, and participation. These components are part of a complex interplay of individual health conditions and environmental factors, which together profoundly influence a person's experience of functioning and disability.

Measuring disability in surveys

Disability is a complex and difficult concept to measure. It is especially difficult to assess the range of disability severity and to capture the full complexity of disability experience in a small number of questions in surveys. In both the Census and surveys, the ABS (2006: 174) defines the profound or severe disability population as: 'those people needing help or assistance in one or more of the three core activity areas of self-care, mobility and communication, because of a long-term health condition (lasting six months or more), a disability (lasting six months or more), or old age'.

'Severity of disability' is a measure often used in surveys. It is based on limitations a person may experience in any tasks relating to the core activities of self-care, communication and mobility. These limitations may be:

- profound – the person always needs help with at least one core activity

- severe – the person needs help with at least one of the core activities some of the time

- moderate – the person has difficulties with at least one of the core activities but does not need assistance, and

- mild – the person uses aids but does not have difficulties with core activities.

An ABS information paper (2010c: 8) on sources of disability information recommends that the most useful measure of disability from surveys is 'profound/ severe core activity limitation', the population for whom service delivery has the most consequence. Unfortunately, the measures of disability proposed by the Productivity Commission for estimating the disability population for the NDIS do not always correspond with those used in these surveys. The NDIS includes four main categories: persons with daily core needs, self-management limitations, psychiatric disabilities, and early intervention.

- 'Persons with daily core needs', are defined as persons whose main condition code is one of a set of assigned conditions and who receive core services at least once daily (based on whether received informally or formally, or required self-care, mobility, or communication assistance at least once daily).

- 'Self-management limitations' is defined as persons whose main condition code is one of a set of assigned conditions and disability status of profound, severe, moderate or mild, or a schooling or work limitation.

- 'Psychiatric disabilities' is defined as persons who need help or supervision in undertaking tasks due to mental illness or condition and have a disability status of profound, severe or moderate, or a schooling or work limitation.

- 'Early intervention' is defined as persons with whose main condition code is one of a set of specified conditions and a disability status of profound, severe, moderate or mild, or a schooling or work limitation.

Despite these limitations, a number of data sources are used to analyse disability. These are described in more detail below. Further information on how persons with a disability were identified in each of these data sources, including the questions that were asked in these surveys, is provided in Appendix 2.

Population Census

Census data from 2006 is used to provide disability prevalence estimates for the Indigenous and non-Indigenous populations by age and region.[1] The 2006 Census collected data on one element of disability: the number of people with a 'core activity need for assistance'. It included four questions which were based on the concept of 'profound or severe core activity limitation'. These questions identified people who had a need for assistance with one or more of the core activity areas of self-care, communication or mobility because of a disability, long-term health condition or the effects of old age.

The 2006 Census enables estimates of disability prevalence (core activity need for assistance) for Indigenous persons of all ages. It should be considered the best source for small area estimates of disability prevalence, and for Indigenous/ non-Indigenous comparisons.

Survey of Disability and Carers

The 2009 Survey of Disability and Carers (SDAC) defines disability as any limitation, restriction or impairment which restricts everyday activities and has lasted or is likely to last for at least six months. It was designed specifically to align with the international measures of disability as described in the ICF. The survey contains 149 questions designed to provide detailed information

---

1   Since the analysis for this monograph was undertaken, some data on disability prevalence from the 2011 Census has been released.

on the identification of disability and the underlying conditions causing disability. The questions address difficulties with sight, hearing, speech and breathing, chronic or recurrent pain, blackouts, fits, learning difficulties, as well as emotional or nervous conditions, physical conditions, disfigurement or deformity, mental illness, head injury, stroke and brain damage.

A series of screening questions are used to establish whether or not any members of a household may have a disability. Where a member of a household meets the SDAC definition of disability, seven criteria are used to determine the severity of the disability. Severity of disability is then classified using the following categories:

- profound core activity limitation
- severe core activity limitation
- moderate core activity limitation
- mild core activity limitation
- education/employment restriction
- no specific limitation or restriction, and long-term health condition.

The SDAC is considered to be the most detailed and comprehensive source of information on disability among the total Australian population (ABS 2010a). However, the sample size for the Indigenous population in the 2009 survey was too small to produce reliable estimates or to support comparative analysis of disability measures by Indigenous/non-Indigenous status (ABS 2010a). The SDAC also does not cover very remote areas of Australia.

National Aboriginal and Torres Strait Islander Social Survey

The 2008 National Aboriginal and Torres Strait Islander Social Survey (NATSISS) collected data on a number of elements of disability using two sets of criteria. A broad set of criteria was used in non-remote areas only, which included sensory, physical and learning difficulties, disfigurements and deformities, conditions which restrict physical activity or physical work, and a nervous or emotional condition and/or mental illness requiring supervision (psychological disability). A common set of criteria were used in both remote and non-remote areas. This measure included the same measures as the broad criteria. However, it does not include people whose only reported disability was psychological.

The disability module used in the NATSISS applies the same criteria as the SDAC to identify people with a disability and determine their severity of restriction, but uses 10 questions and a series of prompt cards. The resulting 'severity of disability' measure allows for the following measures to be ascertained and is intended to be broadly comparable to the same concept in the SDAC:

- profound/severe core activity limitation
- unspecified limitation or restriction
- education/employment restriction only
- no disability or long term health condition.

Disability type is also measured and is categorised according to responses provided concerning the type of condition(s) and whether the condition(s) restricted everyday activities.

The 2008 NATSISS is the most comprehensive source of information on disability for the Indigenous population, and is the only source that collects information on disability type and disability status other than profound/severe disability. However, the information on disability is limited to persons aged 15 years and over and the sample size is not large enough to produce reliable estimates for geographies lower than the State/Territory level. All Australian comparisons are available from the General Social Survey (GSS), although these cover non-remote areas only.

In this monograph, data from the 2008 NATSISS is used to provide detailed information on the types of disability among the Indigenous population and is also compared with 2006 GSS data for all Australians. Data from the 2008 NATSISS is also used to provide information on barriers to accessing services.

Other collections

The National Health Survey includes a disability module, which provides data for the general Australian population: however the comparable Indigenous survey (National Aboriginal and Torres Strait Islander Health Survey (NATSIHS)) does not include such a module for the Indigenous population. It only collects information on whether a person has a long-term health condition; it does not distinguish between those with a long-term health condition that restricts their everyday living (persons considered to have a disability), and those with a long-term health condition without a disability.

The Survey of Education and Training, the Time Use Survey and the National Survey of Mental Health and Wellbeing are other ABS surveys which collect information on severity of disability among the general population.

However, none of these surveys include an Indigenous identifier. Finally, administrative data from the Disability Services National Minimum Data Set (DS NMDS) is used to provide information on users of disability services.

Estimates from the data collections

The strengths and limitations of these collections are outlined in Table 2.1. Further detail on data source gaps and limitations is discussed in Chapter 4.

Table 2.1 Data sources on disability prevalence among the Australian Indigenous population

Data collection	Number of questions related to disability status	Latest collection year	Expected future collections	Data for which the collection is the recommended source	Survey limitations
SDAC	75	2009	2015	Not recommended for Indigenous disability prevalence	Sample size for Indigenous population too small to produce reliable estimates Does not cover very remote areas No small area data
2006 and 2011 Census	4	2011	2016	Prevalence of disability for Indigenous persons of all ages Comparisons of Indigenous and non-Indigenous population Small area data	Only one disability measure is available (need for assistance) which is conceptually related to profound/ severe core activity limitation Non-response rate 6.4% for 'need for assistance', indicating possible response bias
NATSISS	10	2008	2014	Disability status Type of disability measures Relationship between disability and labour force, employment and health characteristics	No small area data Non-Indigenous comparisons only available for non-remote areas using common criteria

Source: Author's analysis

The data collections discussed above employ different methods to identify persons with disability, and use incompatible criteria for classifying a person as having a disability. In addition, the way in which information is collected affects the number of people identified as having a disability. The NATSISS interviewed one adult per household. In the Census, information is collected via a paper questionnaire generally completed by one person on behalf of an entire household. As a consequence, the number and proportion of Indigenous persons with a disability estimated or enumerated varies. It is important to note that the short disability module used in the NATSISS does not separately identify people with a long-term health condition only and without disability. The module does include the concept 'with disability or long term health conditions'. It should also be noted that the surveys considered in the analysis cover different collection periods. However, as prevalence rates only change slowly over time, it is unlikely that this creates a significant margin of error in regard to impact on the identified disability populations.

Table 2.2 Need for assistance compared with severe/profound core activity limitation, Indigenous and all Australians, by age-group, 2006 and 2008

	Needs assistance with core activities (Census 2006)[a]		Severe/profound core activity limitations (NATSISS 2008, GSS 2006)[b]	
Age group	Indigenous	Non-Indigenous	Indigenous Australians (NATSISS 2008)	All Australians (GSS 2006)
0–4	620	10 467	not collected	not collected
5–14	3 025	49 467	not collected	not collected
15–24	4 133	68 096	5 218	15–17 not collected
25–34	1 522	31 911	3 904	62 056
35–44	2 533	51 110	4 223	114 503
45–54	3 116	74 377	4 676	112 025
55–64	2 991	105 588	3 994	188 515

a. Self-reported.

b. Survey administered by interviewer. NATSISS 2008 did not collect disability status 0–14 years, GSS 2006 reports 18 years onward.

Source: AIHW 2011b

For Indigenous persons aged 15 years and over, the number and rate for profound or severe activity limitation was higher for the NATSISS (around 8%) than the Census (6%) (Table 2.2). The number of Indigenous persons with a severe or profound core activity limitation is higher in the 2008 NATSISS than the 2006 Census for all age groups. Similarly, the number of non-Indigenous persons estimated to have severe/profound core activity limitations is higher in the 2006 GSS than the 2006 Census for all age groups. The Indigenous to non-Indigenous rate ratios of severe or profound limitation were fairly consistent between the two surveys, indicating disability rates for Indigenous Australians approximately twice that for non-Indigenous Australians.

A likely explanation for these differences is that while the NATSISS is designed to collect data on the full range of disability severity, the census uses a collapsed question set that specifically targets those with a need for assistance in at least one of the core activity areas. The more the concept of 'need for assistance' is collapsed into a reduced number of questions, the less opportunities there are for people to be identified and correctly categorised, resulting in lower proportions. The census with its four questions produces lower estimates of people being identified as needing assistance with core activities than the NATSISS with its 10 question set.

Profile of disability among Indigenous Australians

This section's disability prevalence data is sourced from the 2006 Census of Population and Housing (Census 2006) and the 2008 NATSISS. Census data is used to provide information on the age profile of Indigenous persons with a disability, and regional analysis on where they live. NATSISS data is used to provide information on disability type and socioeconomic and health characteristics of Indigenous persons with disability.

Number of persons with a disability

According to the 2006 Census, 19 600 Indigenous Australians (4.6%) had a core activity need for assistance, which is conceptually equivalent to severe or profound core activity limitation. After adjusting for differences between the two populations in terms of both age structure and the rate of 'unstated' need for assistance, Indigenous Australians were 1.8 times as likely as non-Indigenous Australians to need assistance with activities of daily living.

Among Indigenous Australians aged under 65 years (15 700), 3.8 per cent had a core activity need for assistance, and were 2.4 times as likely as non-Indigenous Australians of the same age to need assistance with activities of daily living. According to the 2008 NATSISS, around 26 000 Indigenous Australians aged 15 years and over (7.9%) had a severe or profound core activity limitation. This survey however highlights that this group only represents the 'tip of the iceberg' with regard to Indigenous disability and disadvantage. More generally it found that of the total Indigenous population aged 15 years and over almost half (49.8%)—some 163 000 people—had some type of disability or long-term health condition.

Age profile of Indigenous persons with disability

The age profile of the Indigenous disability population may vary depending on the area in which they live, and this may affect the services that are most appropriate for their needs. The age distribution of Indigenous persons who had a core activity need for assistance by remoteness using data from the 2006 Census is shown in Table 2.3. Australia-wide, 18 per cent of the Indigenous disability population were aged 0–14 years, 10 per cent were aged 15–24 years, 21 per cent were aged 25–44 years, 31 per cent were aged 45–64 years, and 20 per cent were aged 65 years and over. The age profile of Indigenous persons requiring assistance with core activities in remote areas was older, with around double the proportion being aged 65 years and over in remote areas compared to regional areas and major cities. Not surprisingly, rates of disability among the total Indigenous population increased with age, with 28 per cent of Indigenous persons aged 65 years and over having a core activity need for assistance.

Table 2.3 Indigenous persons with a core activity need for assistance, by age group and Indigenous status, Australia, 2006

Age group	Needs assistance with core activities (Census 2006)[a]		Severe/profound core activity limitations (NATSISS 2008, GSS 2006)[b]	
	Indigenous	Non-Indigenous	Indigenous Australians (NATSISS 2008)	All Australians (GSS 2006)
0–4	620	10 467	not collected	not collected
5–14	3 025	49 467	not collected	not collected
15–24	4 133	68 096	5 218	15–17 not collected
25–34	1 522	31 911	3 904	62 056
35–44	2 533	51 110	4 223	114 503
45–54	3 116	74 377	4 676	112 025
55–64	2 991	105 588	3 994	188 515

Source: AIHW analysis of 2006 Census data (unpublished)

The ratio of the rate of needing assistance with core activities, for Indigenous and non-Indigenous Australians by age group is shown in Fig. 2.1. The disparity in rates between Indigenous and non-Indigenous is greatest for the 45–54 and 55–64 year age groups, with Indigenous Australians in these age groups being almost three times as likely to require assistance as non-Indigenous Australians. This reflects the pattern of premature ageing seen among the Indigenous population, expressed in a greater chronic disease burden in middle and later life, and shorter life expectancy (Vos et al. 2009).

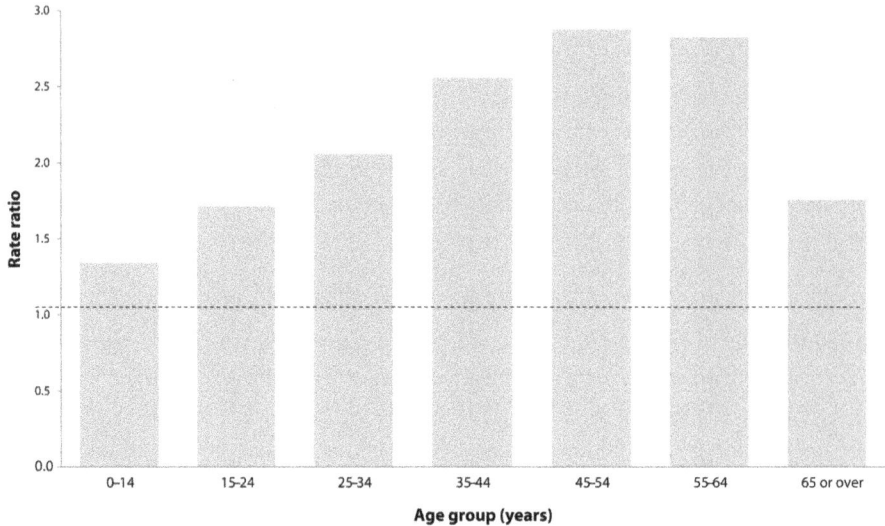

Fig. 2.1 Need for assistance with core activities by Indigenous Australians compared to non-Indigenous Australians, 2006

Based on rates standardised to the age- and sex-distribution of the Australian population.

Excludes people who did not respond to the census questions concerning disability.

A rate ratio greater than 1 means that Indigenous Australians were more likely than non-Indigenous Australians of the same age to need assistance with core activities. Higher rate ratios mean larger differences.

Source: AIHW 2009a; see Appendix Table A5.1

Where do Indigenous people with a disability live?

Of the close to 20 000 Indigenous persons counted in the 2006 Census as needing assistance with core activities, approximately 7 000 (36%) lived in major cities, 9 000 (46%) in regional areas, and 3 500 (18%) in remote/very remote areas. At a State level, differences in the number of Indigenous persons with disability largely reflected differences in the population of each State, with the largest number of Indigenous persons with disability being in New South Wales and Queensland and the smallest number in the Australian Capital Territory and Tasmania (Table 2.4). At the statistical division level, Sydney had the highest numbers of Indigenous persons requiring assistance with core activities, followed by the balance of the Northern Territory, and Brisbane (see Appendix Table A5.2).

Slightly more Aboriginal and Torres Strait Islander people living in major cities and inner regional areas of Australia were suggested by the 2006 Census as needing assistance with a core activity (around 5%), as compared with remote (4%) and very remote areas (3.3%). Rates of disability ranged from 5.7 per cent of Indigenous Australians in Victoria to 3.6 per cent in the Northern Territory.

Reported rates of disability were highest in remote areas of Victoria (31.6%) and lowest in very remote areas of Queensland (2.5%). The Statistical Divisions with the highest proportion of Indigenous persons needing assistance with core activities was Wimmera in Victoria (7.6%), followed by Barton in New South Wales (6.6%) and East Gippsland in Victoria (6.6%).

Table 2.4 Number and proportion of Indigenous persons with a core activity need for assistance, by State/Territory and remoteness, Australia, 2006

	NSW	Vic	Qld	SA	WA	Tas	NT	ACT	Aust
Number of Indigenous persons with a core activity need for assistance									
Major cities	3 074	760	1 574	654	801	na	na	150	7 013
Inner regional	2 294	614	1 152	95	172	486	na	0	4 824
Outer regional	1 218	209	1 309	294	343	355	376	na	4 104
Remote	242	12	315	44	343	25	484	na	1 465
Very remote	37	na	433	155	606	7	883	na	2 121
Total	6 901	1 602	4 806	1 253	2 274	876	1 746	150	19 619
Proportion of Indigenous population with a core activity need for assistance (%)									
Major Cities	5.5	5.5	4.6	5.6	4.3	na	na	4.0	5.1
Inner regional	5.3	6.3	4.7	4.4	4.0	5.7	na	0.0	5.2
Outer regional	5.1	4.8	3.9	5.4	4.3	5.1	4.0	na	4.5
Remote	4.2	31.6	3.2	4.4	4.1	6.5	4.5	na	4.0
Very remote	3.7	na	2.5	4.5	4.2	3.6	3.1	na	3.3
Total	5.3	5.7	4.0	5.3	4.2	5.4	3.6	4.0	4.6
Distribution by State of Indigenous population with core activity need for assistance (%)									
Major cities	44.5	47.4	32.8	52.2	35.2	na	na	100.0	35.7
Inner regional	33.2	38.3	24.0	7.6	7.6	55.5	na	0.0	24.6
Outer regional	17.6	13.0	27.2	23.5	15.1	40.5	21.5	na	20.9
Remote	3.5	0.7	6.6	3.5	15.1	2.9	27.7	na	7.5
Very remote	0.5	na	9.0	12.4	26.6	0.8	50.6	na	10.8
Total	100.0	100.0	100.0	100.0	100.0	100.0	100.0	100.0	100.0

na = combination of State/Territory and remoteness category not defined.

Source: ABS Census of Population and Housing 2006

After adjusting for differences in age structure, Indigenous persons were more likely to require assistance with core activities than non-Indigenous persons in all States and Territories (Fig. 2.2). The greatest disparity in rates was observed in the Northern Territory and Western Australia, with Indigenous Australians just over twice as likely to need assistance with core activities as non-Indigenous Australians. Remote and very remote areas had the greatest disparity in rates of disability, with Indigenous persons 2.3 and 2.5 times more likely than non-Indigenous persons in these areas to have a core activity need for assistance.

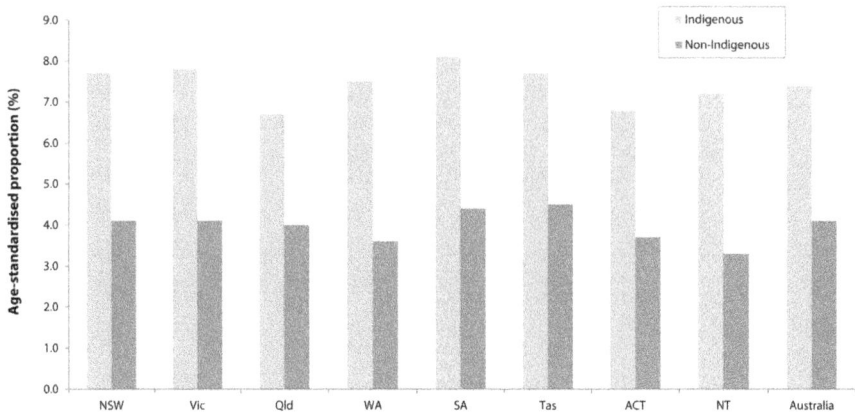

Fig. 2.2 Need for assistance with core activities, by State/Territory and Indigenous status, Australia, 2006

Source: AIHW analysis of 2006 Census (unpublished); Appendix 5 (this volume), Table A5.3

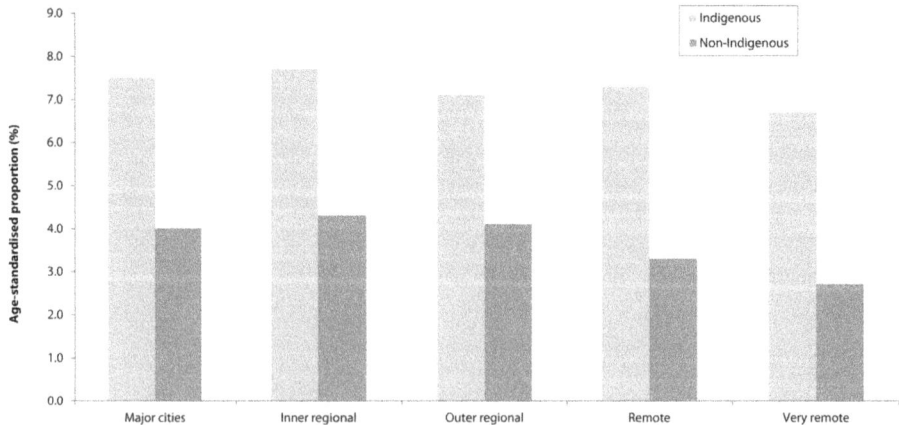

Fig. 2.3 Need for assistance with core activities, by remoteness and Indigenous status, Australia, 2006

Source: AIHW analysis of 2006 Census (unpublished); See Table A5.a

In 2006, 10 per cent of Indigenous Australians who needed assistance with core activities were living in a hospital, residential aged care facility, hostel for the disabled, or other non-private dwelling, compared to 19 per cent of non-Indigenous Australians (ABS and AIHW 2008). This may reflect the very different age profile of the Indigenous population with a disability, as well as the greater spread across the population.

What types of disability are experienced by Indigenous people?

The 2008 NATSISS provides information on the types of disability experienced by Indigenous Australians. Physical disability is the most common type of disability group among Indigenous Australians with severe or profound core activity limitations, consistent with the experience of Australians generally (AIHW 2009a). Among Indigenous Australians aged 15–64 years with severe or profound disability, 82 per cent experience physical disability. Sight, hearing and speech related disability is the next most common among those with severe or profound core activity limitations, at 42 per cent; and around 30 per cent experience intellectual or psychological-related disability (Table 2.5).

Table 2.5 Indigenous Australians aged 15–64 with severe or profound core activity limitations, by disability group, 2008[a]

Disability group (note people can identify multiple groups)[b]	Number	Per cent
Sight, hearing, speech	9 167	41.6
Physical	18 061	82.0
Intellectual	6 362	28.9
Psychological	6 196	28.1
Total	22 015	

a. 2008 NATSISS excluded special dwellings where higher proportions of people with severe and profound disability may be found.

b. The disability types are not mutually exclusive.

Source: AIHW analysis of 2008 NATSISS; AIHW 2011b

According to the 2008 NATSISS, half of all Indigenous Australians aged 15 years and over had some type of disability or long-term health condition. Approximately one-third (33%) were classified as having a physical disability, 17 per cent with sight, hearing or speech impairments, 8 per cent with an intellectual impairment, and 8 per cent with a psychological disability. Rates of intellectual and psychological disability were statistically significantly higher in non-remote than remote areas, while rates of sight, hearing and speech-related disability were significantly higher in remote than non-remote areas (Table 2.6).

Table 2.6 Indigenous Australians aged 15 years and over with disability or long-term health condition, by remoteness, 2008ᵃ

Disability type	Remote (%)	Non-remote (%)	Total (%)
Sight, hearing, speech	21.1*	15.7*	17.0
Physical	30.5	33.3	32.6
Intellectual	3.8*	9.0*	7.7
Psychological	5.1*	8.7*	7.8
Type not specified	22.6	25.0	24.4
Total with a disability or long-term health condition	48.8	50.2	49.8
No disability or long-term health condition	51.2	49.8	50.2
Total	100.0	100.0	100.0

a. Data presented in this table are limited to the common set of criteria used in remote and non-remote areas. Data are therefore not comparable with 2002 or 2008 NATSISS data for people in non-remote areas only, nor with disability data from the 2002 GSS or 2007–08 National Health Survey (NHS).

* Statistically significant difference at the 5% level of significance in the remote/non-remote comparisons.

Source: AIHW analysis of 2008 NATSISS; Steering Committee for the Review of Government Service Provision (SCRGSP) 2011)

While rates of physical disability and sight, hearing and speech impairment increased with age among Indigenous persons aged 15 years and over, rates of intellectual and psychological-related disability were fairly similar across all age groups (Fig. 2.4).

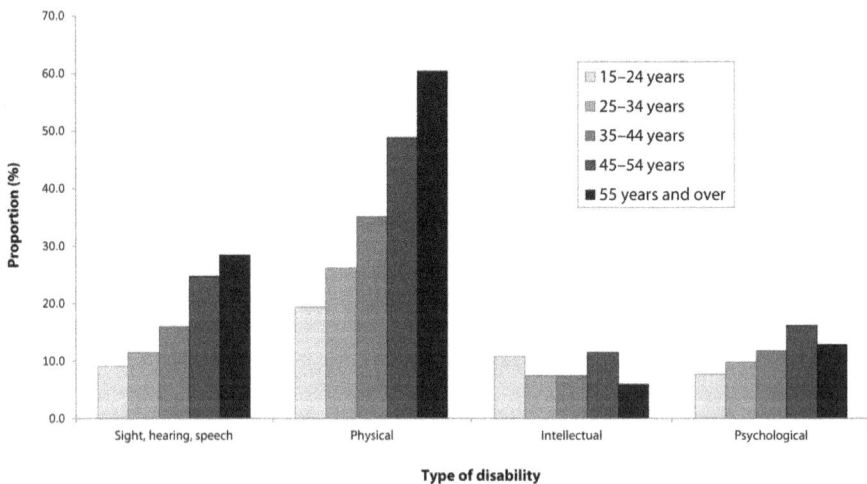

Fig. 2.4 Type of disability, Indigenous persons aged 15 years and over in non-remote areas, by age group, Australia, 2008

Source: 2008 NATSISS; see Appendix Table A5.5

Information on disability type for the non-Indigenous population is available from the 2006 GSS for non-remote areas only. After adjusting for differences in age structure between the Indigenous and non-Indigenous populations, Indigenous persons living in non-remote areas had higher rates of disability than non-Indigenous Australians living in non-remote areas for all types of disability except for sight, hearing and speech impairment, for which rates were similar for the two population groups. The greatest disparity in rates was for intellectual disability, for which rates were 3.2 times higher among the Indigenous population.

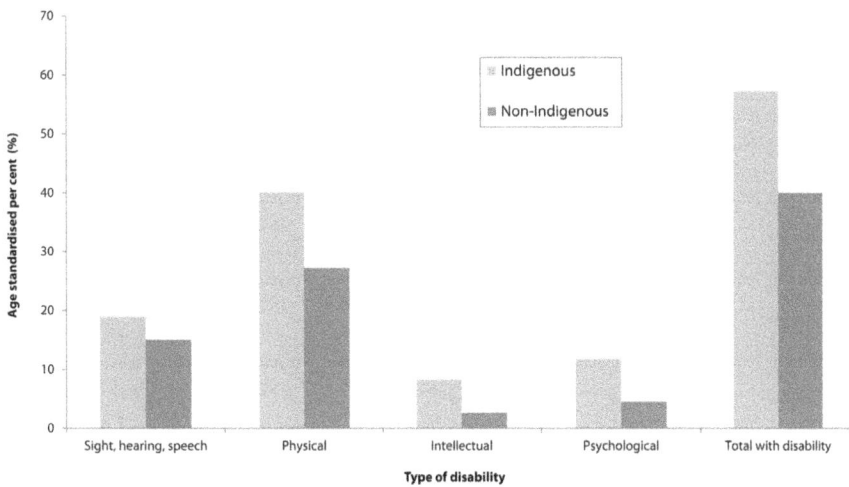

Fig. 2.5 Persons aged 15 years and over in non-remote areas, by type of disability, Australia, 2006 (non-Indigenous) and 2008 (Indigenous)

Source: 2008 NATSISS and 2006 GSS; see Appendix Table A5.5

Impact on education and employment

The 2008 NATSISS collected additional information from Indigenous persons who were classified as having a disability, on whether they had an education or employment restriction due to disability. Approximately 5 per cent of Indigenous persons aged 15–64 years with a disability were classified as having an education restriction due to disability, and 16 per cent were classified as having an employment restriction (Table 2.7 and Table 2.8). Rates of education restriction were highest among those aged 15–24 years (14.4%). Rates of employment restriction were highest among those aged 45–54 years (19.7%).

Table 2.7 Indigenous persons with a disability or long-term health condition aged 15–64 years, by education restriction due to disability and age group, Australia, 2008

Age group	Has an education restriction due to disability		Does not have an education restriction due to disability		Total with a disability	
	No.	%	No.	%	No.	%
15–24	5 339	14.4	31 775	85.6	37 113	100.0
25–34	907	3.0	28 896	97.0	29 803	100.0
35–44	479	1.5	32 382	98.5	32 862	100.0
45–54	532	1.7	30 682	98.3	31 214	100.0
55–64	310	1.5	19 965	98.5	20 275	100.0
Total	7 567	5.0	143 701	95.0	151 267	100.0

Source: AIHW analysis of 2008 NATSISS (unpublished data)

Table 2.8 Indigenous persons with a disability or long-term health condition aged 15–64 years, by employment restriction due to disability, and age group, Australia, 2008

Age group	Has an education restriction due to disability		Does not have an education restriction due to disability		Total with a disability	
	No.	%	No.	%	No.	%
15–24	5 339	14.4	31 775	85.6	37 113	100.0
25–34	907	3.0	28 896	97.0	29 803	100.0
35–44	479	1.5	32 382	98.5	32 862	100.0
45–54	532	1.7	30 682	98.3	31 214	100.0
55–64	310	1.5	19 965	98.5	20 275	100.0
Total	7 567	5.0	143 701	95.0	151 267	100.0

Source: AIHW analysis of 2008 NATSISS (unpublished data)

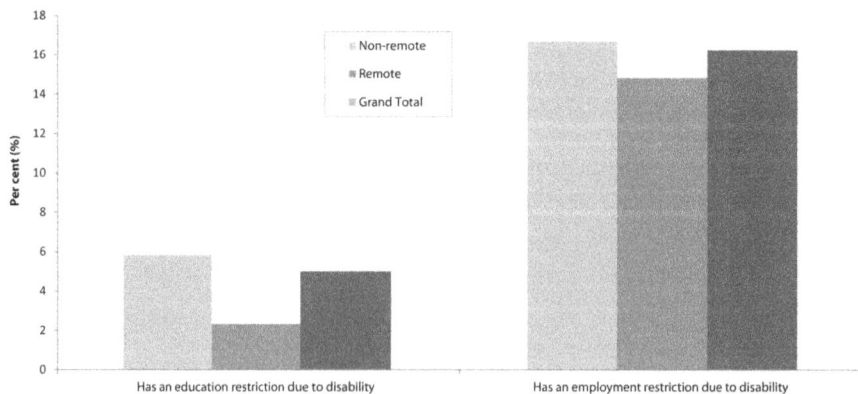

Fig. 2.6 Education or employment restriction due to disability, Indigenous persons aged 15–64 years, Australia, 2008

Source: AIHW analysis of 2008 NATSISS; see Appendix Table A5.6

A higher proportion of Indigenous persons with disability living in non-remote areas had an education restriction compared to those living in remote areas (5.8% compared to 2.3%). The proportion of Indigenous persons who had an employment restriction due to disability was similar for remote and non-remote areas. Interpreting this data is somewhat difficult due to the fact that educational restrictions only tend to be identified in the case of individuals for whom education may be seen as an option. This data may thus be affected by low levels of educational participation and aspirations. In addition the NATSISS does not contain data in this regard for those aged under 15 years.

Has disability among the Indigenous population changed over time?

The 2002 NATSISS provides some comparable data on disability with the 2008 NATSISS, based on the common criteria used in remote and non-remote areas.

The prevalence of severe or profound core activity limitation remained fairly stable between 2002 (7.7%) and 2008 (7.9%) among Indigenous Australians in remote or non-remote areas (Table 2.9). Data indicates the possibility of an increase in rates of 'disability /restriction not defined' and 'total with disability or long-term health condition', in both remote and non-remote areas. Rates of disability or long-term health conditions increased from 35 per cent to 49 per cent in remote areas, and from 37 per cent to 50 per cent in non-remote areas.

Table 2.9 Severity of disability, Indigenous Australians aged 15 years and over by remoteness, 2002 and 2008[a]

	Remote (%)	Non-remote (%)	Total (%)
2002			
Total with profound/severe core activity restriction	8.9	7.3	7.7
Disability/restriction not defined	26.5*	29.6*	28.7*
Total with disability or long-term health condition	35.4*	36.9*	36.5*
2008			
Profound/severe core activity restriction	8.1	7.9	7.9
Disability/restriction not defined	40.7*	42.3*	41.9*
Total with disability or long-term health condition	48.8*	50.2*	49.8*

a. Data presented in this table are limited to the common set of criteria used in remote and non-remote areas. Data are therefore not comparable with 2002 or 2008 NATSISS data for people in non-remote areas only, nor with disability data from the 2002 GSS or 2007–08 NHS.

*Statistically significant difference in the 2002 and 2008 comparisons at the 5% level of significance.

Source: 2002 and 2008 NATSISS; SCRGSP 2011

Socioeconomic characteristics of Indigenous persons with a disability

Income

Financial circumstances strongly influence the degree to which an individual with disability can participate in society. People with disability tend to have fewer financial resources than those without disability. Figure 2.7 gives the per cent of the Indigenous population both with and without a disability who fall into each of the five income quintiles, calculated using the distribution of the total population. While both groups are under-represented in the highest income quintiles (reflecting the lower income of Indigenous compared to non-Indigenous households), those with severe or profound core activity limitations are much more likely to be found in lower income households than those without a disability. Among Aboriginal and Torres Strait Islander peoples in the 25–54 years age groups, the median income for those who needed assistance with a core activity was around 60 per cent of that for Indigenous Australians who did not need assistance.

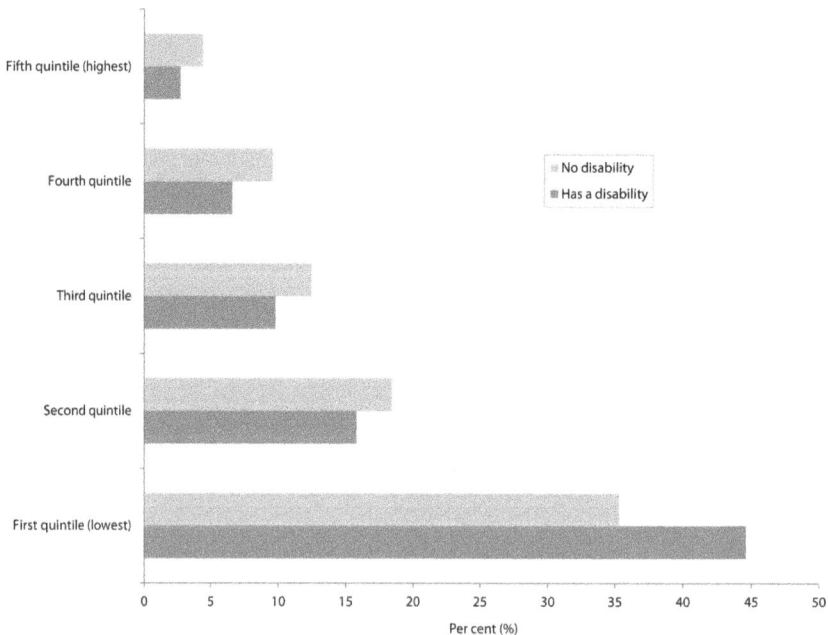

Fig. 2.7 Disability status by equivalised gross household income, Aboriginal and Torres Strait Islander people aged 15 years and over, Australia, 2008ᵃ.

a. Total with a disability or long-term health condition as determined by the common (remote + non-remote) criteria.

Source: 2008 NATSISS; ABS 2011; see Appendix Table A5.7

Employment

The level of employment among Indigenous Australians aged 15–64 years with core activity assistance needs was only about one-quarter that of other Indigenous Australians of the same age (13% and 51% respectively) (AIHW 2011b). Of Aboriginal and Torres Strait Islander people aged 15–64 years reporting core activity limitations, 80 per cent were not in the labour force, compared with 38 per cent of those not reporting core activity limitations.

Although employment levels were higher, a similar pattern was evident among non-Indigenous people aged 15–64 years, where 17 per cent of those with a need for assistance were employed, compared with 73 per cent of those without need for assistance (Table 2.10).

Table 2.10 Employment status by Indigenous status and need for assistance, Indigenous and non-Indigenous Australians aged 15–64 years, 2006

Employment status	Need for assistance		No need for assistance	
	Indigenous	Non-Indigenous	Indigenous	Non-Indigenous
	Proportion of the population (%)			
Employed	12.9	16.5	51.3	73.2
Unemployed	3.4	2.5	9.4	3.9
Not in the labour force	83.7	81.0	39.3	22.9
Sub-total: not participating in the labour force	87.1	83.5	48.7	26.8
Total persons (no.)	11 592	285 198	230 723	11 711 602

Source: AIHW 2011b

These data suggest that disability strongly influences employment outcomes among Indigenous people, to a degree similar to that experienced by non-Indigenous people with the same severity of disability.

Source of income

With such low employment it is not surprising that there is a much greater reliance on government pensions and allowances among Indigenous Australians with severe or profound disability. Nearly two-thirds (64%) of Indigenous Australians aged 18–64 years with severe or profound core activity limitations relied on government pensions and allowances as their principal source of income: double that of Indigenous Australians without disability or long term health conditions (32%) (Table 2.11).

The 2006 GSS of all Australians found 56 per cent of those aged 18–64 years with severe or profound disability relied on government pensions and allowances as their principal source of income, compared with 10 per cent of those without disability (Table 2.11).

Table 2.11 Principal source of income by disability level and Indigenous status, Australia, 2006 and 2008[a]

Principal source of income	Severe or profound core activity limitations		No disability or long-term health conditions	
	Indigenous Australians (%)	All Australians (%)	Indigenous Australians (%)	All Australians (%)
Employee income	20.2	20.2	50.9	66.7
Government pensions & allowances	64.4	56.3	31.9	9.9
Other[b]	15.4	23.5	17.2	23.4
Total persons (no.)	20 721	516 487	135 441	8 477 923

a. Includes unincorporated business income, CDEP income, investment income, other income and undefined.

b. 2008 NATSISS and 2006 GSS excluded special dwellings where higher proportions of people with disability may be found, and 2006 GSS excluded very remote and sparsely settled areas.

Source: AIHW analysis of 2008 NATSISS and 2006 GSS; AIHW 2011b

These findings are consistent with 2006 Census data indicating that people with disability are clustered at the lower-income levels. The income patterns for Indigenous and non-Indigenous Australians with disability are very similar, reinforcing the suggestion that there is a strong relationship between income and disability.

Education

Education plays a significant role in developing the skills and abilities of people with disability; supporting them in their learning goals, providing a foundation for breaking free from the type of entrenched disadvantage financial hardship causes, and fostering their participation in Australian society (AIHW 2009a; National People with Disabilities and Carer Council 2009). As seen in Fig. 2.8 (from AIHW 2011b), Year 12 attainment rates were much lower among 18–64 year old Indigenous Australians with severe or profound disability (16%), compared with Indigenous Australians without disability (28%). The rates for all Australians are significantly higher and the 2006 GSS showed that 31 per cent of all Australians with more severe disability and 58 per cent of those without disability completed Year 12. Of particular note is that an estimated 45 per cent of Indigenous Australians aged 18–64 years with severe or profound disability left school at Year 9 or below, almost double that of other Indigenous Australians (24%). This pattern is even more pronounced among the Australian population generally.

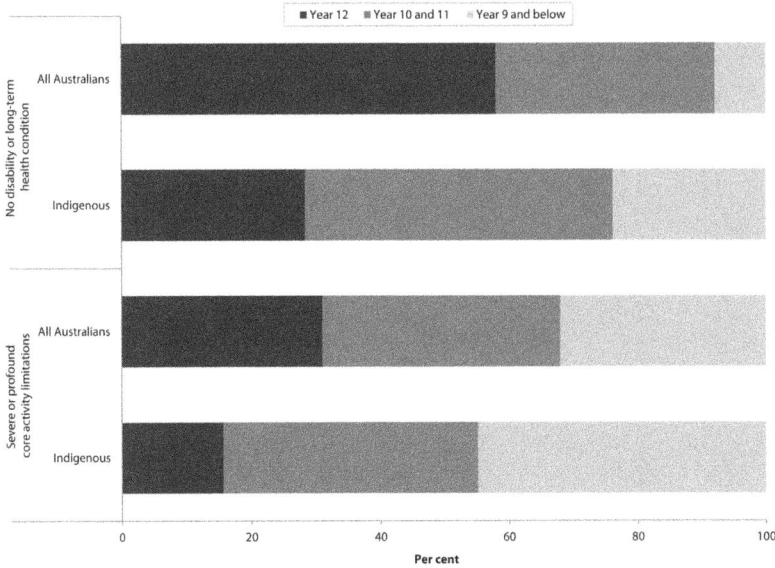

Fig. 2.8 Highest school attainment, by disability and Indigenous status, age 18–64 years, 2006 and 2008[a]

a. 2008 NATSISS and 2006 GSS excluded special dwellings where higher proportions of people with disability may be found and 2006 GSS excluded very remote and sparsely settled areas.

Source: AIHW analysis of 2008 NATSISS and 2006 GSS; AIHW 2011b; see Appendix Table A5.8

Just under one-third (30%) of Indigenous Australians aged 18–64 years with severe or profound core activity limitations had an interest in further study in the 12 months preceding the survey. This is slightly higher than Indigenous people without disability in the same age range (27%). The most frequently cited reason among Indigenous Australians with severe or profound disability for not studying further was personal caring and other family reasons (see Appendix Table A5.9).

The health and wellbeing of Indigenous persons with a disability

Self-assessed health status

While self-assessed health status is a subjective measure, perceptions of health are important to mental and physical wellbeing. As Fig. 2.9 reveals, Indigenous Australians with severe or profound core activity limitations are far more likely to assess their health as fair or poor (59%) than Indigenous Australians without disability (8%). This is consistent with the pattern seen among the Australian population generally, where 55 per cent of all people with severe or profound disability assess their health as fair or poor compared with 3 per cent of all people without disability. Among Indigenous Australians without disability, perceptions of health are more closely aligned with those of Australians without disability than with Indigenous Australians with severe or profound disability (Fig. 2.9).

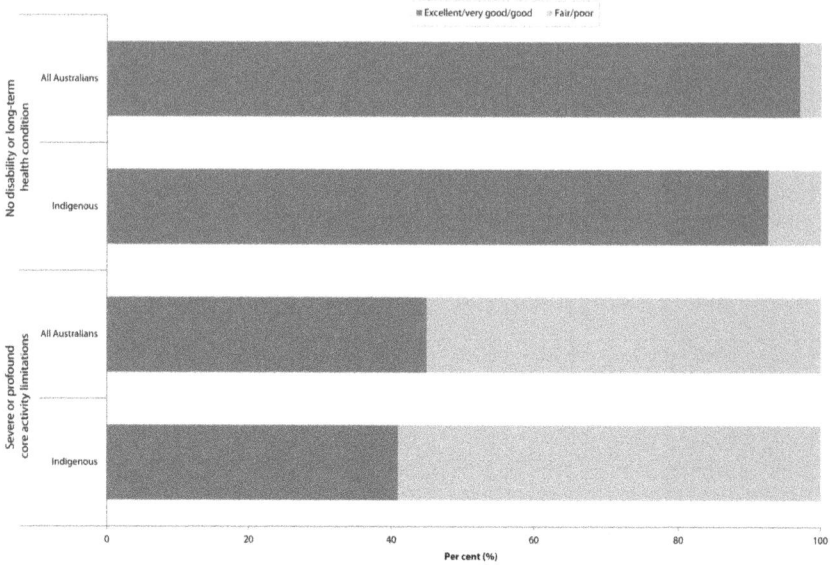

Fig. 2.9 Self-assessed health, by disability and Indigenous status, age 18–64 years, Australia, 2006 and 2008[a]

2008 NATSISS and 2006 GSS excluded special dwellings where higher proportions of people with disability may be found and 2006 GSS excluded very remote and sparsely settled areas.

Source: AIHW analysis of 2008 NATSISS and 2006 GSS; AIHW 2011b; see Appendix Table A5.10

Stressors

Stressors have a significant impact on quality of life and over time and may influence mental and physical wellbeing. They include stressful life events such as divorce, domestic violence, losing one's job, and overcrowding at home. Along with lower perceptions of health, Indigenous Australians with severe or profound core activity limitations experience such events at greater rates than other Indigenous Australians (Fig. 2.10). This is consistent with findings of the 2007–08 National Health Survey (NHS), that among all Australians, people with a disability are more likely than those without disability to experience stressful life events.

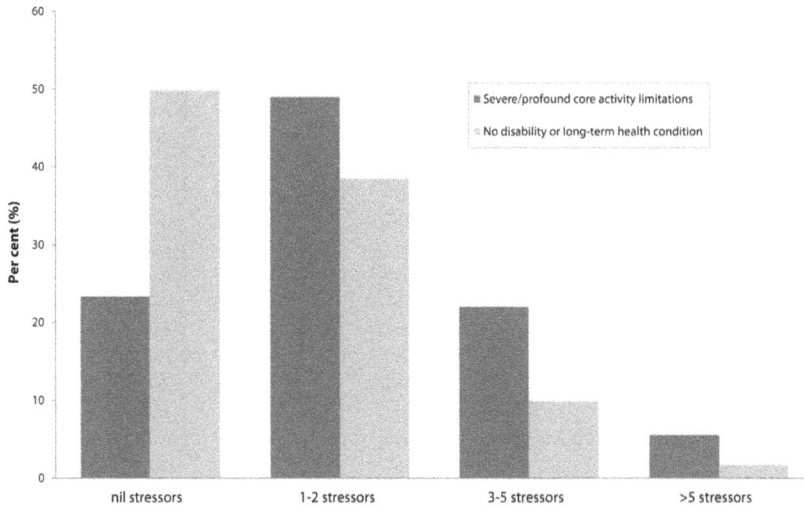

Fig. 2.10 Number of stressors experienced in the previous 12 months, Indigenous Australians, 2008[a]

a. 2008 NATSISS included remote, very remote and indigenous communities but excluded special dwellings where higher proportions of people with severe and profound disability may be found.

Source: AIHW analysis of 2008 NATSISS; AIHW 2011b; see Appendix Table A5.11

Health risk factors

It has been reported elsewhere that Indigenous Australians are more likely than non-Indigenous Australians to be smokers, and that among Australians generally, people with a disability are more likely than those without a disability to smoke (AIHW 2011b). Consistent with this evidence, the 2008 NATSISS shows that Indigenous Australians aged 15–64 years with severe or profound core activity limitations have higher rates of daily smoking (52%), compared with Indigenous Australians without disability (42%). The latest ABS figures suggest that Indigenous Australians aged 15 years and over were twice as likely as non-Indigenous people to be current daily smokers (ABS 2010c). Rates of risky alcohol consumption and substance use have also been found to be slightly higher among Australians aged 15–64 years who have severe or profound disability (AIHW 2011a). However, this pattern is not seen among Indigenous Australians (Table 2.12).

Table 2.12 Indigenous Australians aged 15–64 years, health risk factors by disability status, 2008[a]

Factor	Severe/profound core activity limitations		No disability or long-term health conditions	
	No.	%	No.	%
Smoker daily	11 380	52	67 989	42
Medium to high risk alcohol consumption	3 134	14	26 893	17
Substance use in last 12 months	4 665	21	32 181	20
Total	22 015	100	160 990	100

a. 2008 NATSISS included remote, very remote and indigenous communities but excluded special dwellings where higher proportions of people with severe and profound disability may be found.

Source: AIHW analysis of 2008 NATSISS; AIHW 2011b

3. Disability support services: Indigenous users and barriers to access

Individuals with disability, both Indigenous and non-Indigenous, have general needs which can be met by accessing mainstream services. However, people with severe or profound disability often have unique needs that can more appropriately be met by specialist disability services. The purpose of such services is to support and enhance the participation of individuals with disability in their communities in ways that are most effective for the individual. In particular, the purpose of specialist disability services funded under the National Disability Agreement (NDA) is that 'people with disability and their carers have an enhanced quality of life and participate as valued members of the community' (Council of Australian Governments (COAG) n.d.). The NDA was formerly the Commonwealth State/Territory Disability Agreement (CSTDA).

Information on Indigenous persons accessing mainstream disability services can be obtained from the Disability Services National Minimum Data Set (DS NMDS), formerly the CSTDA NMDS, which is held by the Australian Institute of Health and Welfare (AIHW). In this monograph, we focus on differences by State/Territory. However, it should be noted that data from the DS NMDS can potentially be analysed at lower levels of geography. The DS NMDS collects information on services and service users where funding has been provided, during the specified period, by a government organisation operating under the NDA.

As this research presents data collected under both the CSTDA and the NDA, the following terminology will be used:

- CSTDA NMDS refers to the National Minimum Data Set for years up to 2008–09

- the CSTDA NMDS was renamed the Disability Services National Minimum Data Set (DS NMDS) from 1 July 2009

- CSTDA/NDA refers to both agreements under which the data was collected

- 'disability support services' refers to services provided under both CSTDA and NDA.

Disability service users by geography

In 2009–10 there were 14 251 Indigenous people who used specialist disability services funded under the NDA. However, this figure may be understated because of the high number of service users (16 442) for whom Indigenous status is not stated.

The number of Indigenous service users increased from 7 182 to 14 251 between 2005–06 and 2009–10, with increases in most States and Territories (Fig. 3.1). While there was also an increase in the number of non-Indigenous service users over the period (Fig. 3.2) from 186 805 to 264 331, proportionally a much greater share of service users were identified as Indigenous at the end of the period compared to the start. Part of this is driven by the decrease over this period in the rates of Indigenous status recorded as 'not stated/not collected', which have fallen from 10 per cent in 2005–06 to around 5 per cent in 2009–10.

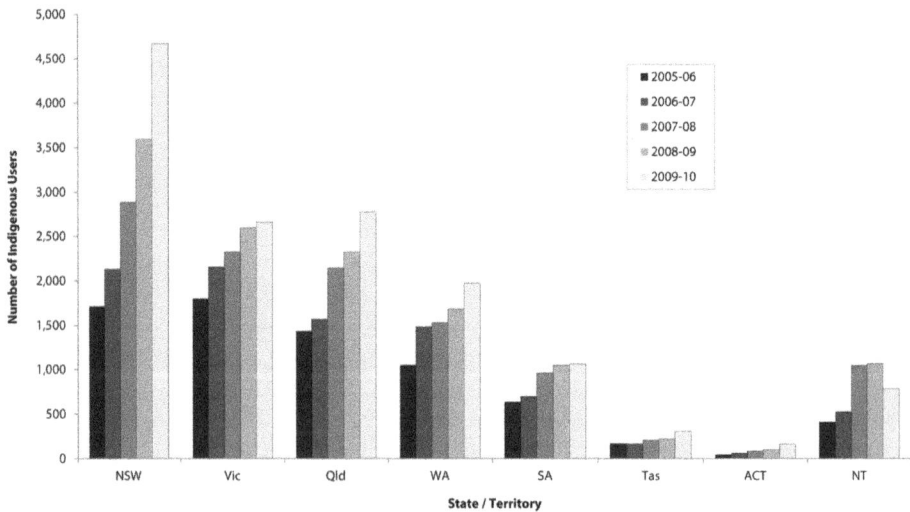

Fig. 3.1 Disability support services, Indigenous service users, by State/ Territory, Australia, 2005–06 to 2009–10[a]

Service user data are estimates after use of a statistical linkage key to account for individuals who received services from more than one service type outlet during the 12-month period. Data for the Northern Territory was under-enumerated in 2009–10. Please exercise caution when comparing 2009-10 Northern Territory data with data from other years.

Source: AIHW analysis of DS NMDS 2005–06 to 2009–10; see Appendix Table A15.2

The highest proportion of Indigenous service users are aged 25–44 years (29%) followed by those aged 15–24 years (25%) (Table 3.1). The median age of Indigenous users of disability support services is 25 years, compared to 34 years for non-Indigenous Australians.

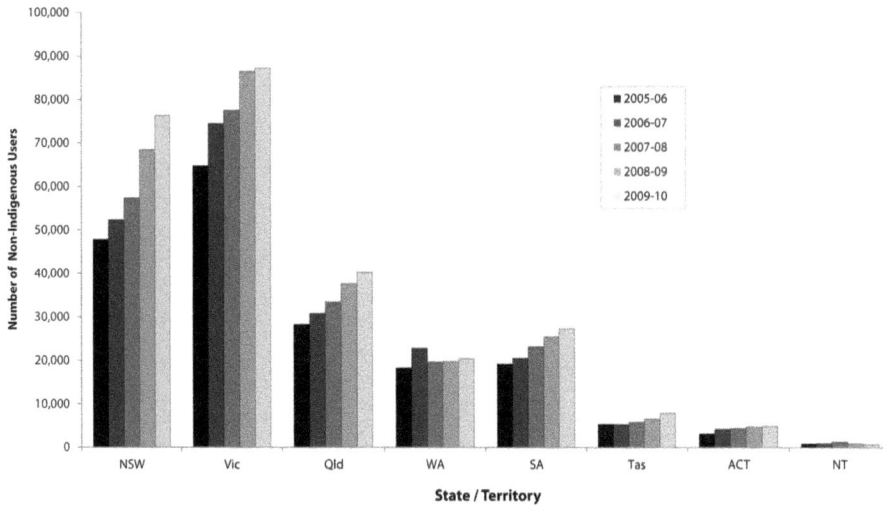

Fig. 3.2 Disability support services, non-Indigenous service users, by State/Territory, Australia, 2005–06 to 2009–10[a]

a. Service user data are estimates after use of a statistical linkage key to account for individuals who received services from more than one service type outlet during the 12 month period.

Source: AIHW analysis of DS NMDS 2005–06 to 2009–10; see Appendix Table A5.18

Table 3.1 Users of disability support services, by Indigenous status and age group, Australia, 2009–10

Age group	Indigenous		Non-Indigenous		Not stated/not collected		Total		Proportion Indigenous (%)[a]
	No.	%	No.	%	No.	%	No.	%	
0–4	1 065	7.5	18 290	6.9	888	5.4	20 243	6.9	5.5
5–14	2 471	17.3	32 281	12.2	2 681	16.3	37 433	12.7	7.1
15–24	3 526	24.7	45 718	17.3	2 771	16.9	52 015	17.6	7.2
25–44	4 191	29.4	80 771	30.6	4 043	24.6	89 005	30.2	4.9
45–54	1 691	11.9	43 361	16.4	1 768	10.8	46 820	15.9	3.8
55–64	929	6.5	29 173	11.0	1 400	8.5	31 502	10.7	3.1
65+	378	2.7	14 737	5.6	2 891	17.6	18 006	6.1	2.5
Total	14 251	100	264 331	100	16 442	100	295 024	100	5.1
Median age	25.0	–	34.0	–	34.0	–	33.0		

a. The final column gives the proportion of the relevant age group who identify as being Indigenous.

Source: AIHW 2011b; see Appendix Table A5.15

Of all Indigenous service users of disability support services in 2009–10, 39 per cent lived in major cities, compared to 64 per cent of non-Indigenous service users. Around 46 per cent lived in regional areas, and 13 per cent lived in remote or very remote areas (Table 3.2).

Table 3.2 Users of disability support services, by Indigenous status and location, Australia, 2009–10

Remoteness area	Indigenous		Non-Indigenous		Not stated/ not collected		Total		Proportion Indigenous (%)[a]
	No.	%	No.	%	No.	%	No.	%	
Major cities	5 550	38.9	170 084	64.3	9 797	59.6	185 430	62.9	3.2
Inner regional	3 828	26.9	62 987	23.8	3 352	20.4	70 167	23.8	5.7
Outer regional	2 743	19.2	23 279	8.8	957	5.8	26 978	9.1	10.5
Remote	877	6.2	2 198	0.8	54	0.3	3 129	1.1	28.5
Very remote	989	6.9	534	0.2	11	0.1	1 533	0.5	64.9
Not stated/ not collected	264	1.9	5 249	2.0	2 271	13.8	7 787	2.6	4.8
Total	14 251	100.0	264 331	100.0	16 442	100.0	295 024	100.0	5.1

a. The final column gives the proportion of the relevant age group who identify as being Indigenous.

Source: AIHW analysis of DS NMDS 2009–10; AIHW 2011b

Disability groups

Intellectual disability is the most common primary disability type among Indigenous service users (34%), followed by physical disability (18%) and psychiatric disability (16%). The proportion of disability groups among Indigenous and non-Indigenous Australians was similar except for intellectual which was higher for Indigenous persons (34% compared to 29%) and vision which was lower for Indigenous persons (2% compared to 5% for non-Indigenous) (Table 3.3).

Table 3.3 Characteristics of Indigenous and non-Indigenous service users of disability support services, Australia, 2009–10

Primary disability group	Indigenous		Non-Indigenous		Not stated/ not collected		Total		Proportion Indigenous (%)[a]
	No.	%	No.	%	No.	%	No.	%	
Intellectual	4 809	33.7	77 515	29.3	1 467	8.9	83 791	28.4	5.8
Specific learning/ADD[b]	667	4.7	9 818	3.7	122	0.7	10 607	3.6	6.4
Autism	673	4.7	17 920	6.8	382	2.3	18 975	6.4	3.6
Physical	2 513	17.6	45 244	17.1	759	4.6	48 516	16.4	5.3
Acquired brain injury	772	5.4	10 172	3.8	357	2.2	11 301	3.8	7.1
Neurological	491	3.4	11 845	4.5	464	2.8	12 800	4.3	4.0
Deaf/blind	36	0.3	625	0.2	18	0.1	679	0.2	5.4
Vision	256	1.8	12 119	4.6	2 677	16.3	15 052	5.1	2.1
Hearing	246	1.7	5 498	2.1	702	4.3	6 446	2.2	4.3
Speech	211	1.5	2 968	1.1	133	0.8	3 312	1.1	6.6
Psychiatric	2 258	15.8	47 376	17.9	2 699	16.4	52 333	17.7	4.5
Developmental delay	539	3.8	8 190	3.1	298	1.8	9 027	3.1	6.2
Not stated/ not collected	780	5.5	15 041	5.7	6 364	38.7	22 185	7.5	4.9
Total	14 251	100.0	264 331	100.0	16 442	100.0	295 024	100.0	5.1

a. The final column gives the proportion of the relevant age group who identify as being Indigenous.

b. ADD = attention deficit disorder

Source: AIHW analysis of DS NMDS 2009–10; AIHW 2011b

Type of assistance provided

The DS NMDS classifies types of services provided by disability services into five broad categories: community support, community access, accommodation support, respite, and employment. In 2009–10, community support was the most commonly used service type among Indigenous service users (54%), followed by employment support (34%), community access (15%), respite (15%) and accommodation support (14%) (Fig. 3.3).

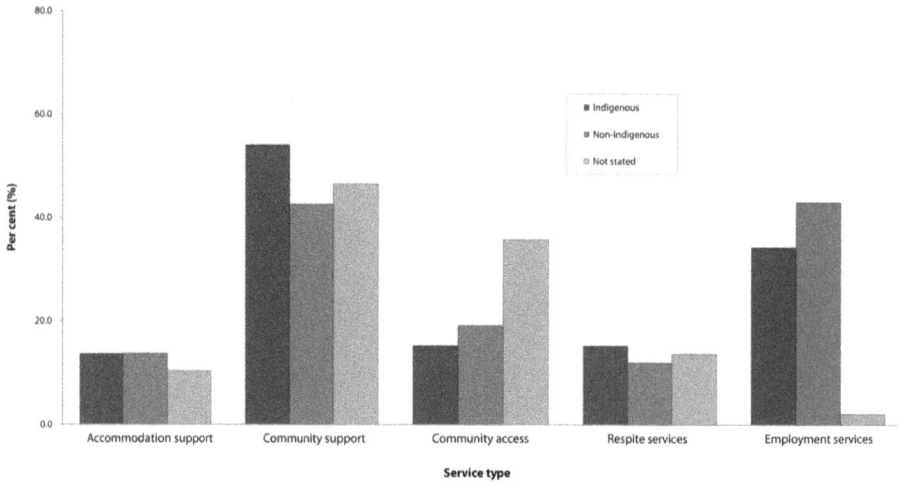

Fig. 3.3 Users of disability support services by type and Indigenous status, Australia, 2009–10ᵃ

a. Service user data are estimates after use of a statistical linkage key to account for individuals who use more than one service.

Source: AIHW analysis of DS NMDS 2009–10; see Appendix Table A5.13

Community support services include individual therapy, early childhood intervention, case management, behaviour management and counselling. Case management was the main community support service used by Indigenous service users at a rate of 29 per cent, followed by therapy support at 12 per cent (see Appendix Table A5.15). Case management is used in care planning and/or to facilitate access to appropriate services.

Community access services include learning/life skills development, recreation/ holiday programs and other community access. Indigenous service users used learning/life skills development at a rate of 12 per cent, and used other community access at a rate of 4 per cent.

Respite services include centre-based services, flexible respite, and own home/ host family and other respite. Flexible respite was the main community respite service used by Indigenous Australians at 10 per cent, which was higher than for non-Indigenous service users (7%).

Accommodation support services include residential institutions, hostels and group homes; personal care and in-home support; and alternative family placement and other accommodation services. Personal care and in-home support was the most common accommodation support service used by Indigenous Australians, which was slightly higher than for non-Indigenous service users (8% compared to 7% respectively). Use of residential institutions, hostels and group homes by Indigenous Australians was slightly lower than for non-Indigenous service users (5% compared to 6%) (Appendix Table A5.14).

Employment services include open employment services which assist people with disability to find or retain employment in the open job market. Almost one-third (30%) of Indigenous service users received open employment services compared with 36 per cent of non-Indigenous users.

The proportion of Indigenous users accessing accommodation support and community access has decreased over the past five years, while use of employment services has increased. In 2008–09, there was an increase in respite use, although the overall trend of this service use is downward (Fig. 3.4).

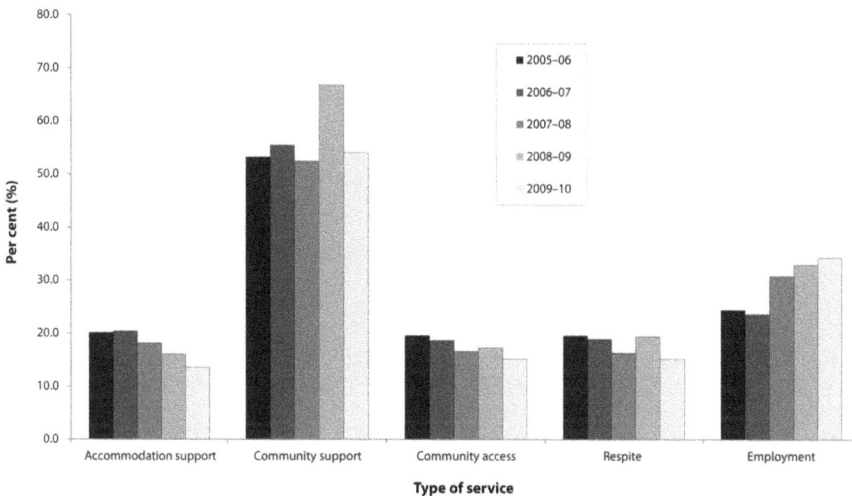

Fig. 3.4 Indigenous users of disability support services, by type, Australia, 2005–06 to 2009–10[a]

a. Service user data are estimates after use of a statistical linkage key to account for individuals who use more than one service.

Source: AIHW analysis of DS NMDS 2005–06, 2007–08, 2008–09, 2009–10; see Appendix Table A5.16

Amount of assistance provided by disability support services

In 2009–10, the average number of hours of assistance provided to Indigenous disability support service users was very similar to that which was provided to non-Indigenous users (13.3 and 12.8 hours respectively). However, the amount of assistance provided to Indigenous and non-Indigenous users varied by service type. For example, 41 mean hours were provided to Indigenous users in accommodation support, more than 1.5 times higher than that provided to non-Indigenous users (26 hours) (see Appendix Table A5.17).

Average hours of support received by Indigenous users varied across remoteness categories in each of the service groups, while the amount of assistance received by non-Indigenous users was relatively consistent across remoteness categories. Average hours of respite assistance provided to Indigenous users varied from 6.7 hours in remote/very remote areas to 9 hours in major city areas. Non-Indigenous users received an average of 8.5 hours of respite assistance. Accommodation support assistance for Indigenous users was the highest in Outer Regional areas with the mean of 48 hours. This assistance for non-Indigenous users was the highest in remote/very remote areas, with a mean of 30 hours (see Appendix Table A5.17).

Income and employment status of Indigenous specialist disability service users

In 2009–10, the main income source for the majority of Indigenous disability support service users aged 16 years and over was from a disability support pension (60.1%). This was followed by 'other pension/benefit' (21.9%) and paid employment (5.1%), while 3.5 per cent had no source of income (see Appendix Table A5.18). Approximately 19.7 per cent of Indigenous service users aged 15 years and over were employed, 37.5 per cent were unemployed, and 36.9 per cent were not in the labour force (see Appendix Table A5.18).

Met need for disability support services

Information on the rate of Indigenous people with disability receiving disability services has been estimated by the AIHW for the years 2007–09 onwards by applying rates of profound/severe disability from the SDAC to Indigenous population projections in order to derive a 'potential population' of Indigenous persons with disability. These data have been used to report against the Performance benchmark in the National Disability Agreement which seeks '[a]n increase in the proportion of Indigenous people with disability receiving disability services'.

Rates of disability service use per potential population are estimated for persons aged 0–64 years, as this is considered to be the target population of persons accessing disability support services. Persons with disability aged 65 years and over will mostly access aged-care services for support.

The AIHW reports that in 2011 there were 413 Indigenous service users per 1 000 potential population, compared with 382 non-Indigenous service users per 1 000 potential population for 2009–10. While this suggests that overall the relative level of Indigenous access was commensurate with the non-Indigenous population this result does not appear to be consistent across the population. In particular, as discussed later, this appears to be primarily driven by outcomes for the 15–24 year age group, with all other age groups showing relatively lower rates of Indigenous access.

Further analysis of service data against potential population estimates reveals some State/Territory based variations, although caution should be exercised in interpreting these data as service models vary across jurisdictions and may affect comparability.

Data for 2009–10 suggest that while New South Wales and Queensland have the largest populations of Indigenous people with severe or profound core activity limitations, according to the potential population estimates their rates of service provision to Indigenous service users per 1 000 population fall slightly below the Australian average. Indigenous under-identification may have influenced this rate, as the number of service users with Indigenous status recorded as 'not stated/not collected' is over 2 000 in New South Wales and around 1 000 in Queensland. Victoria has the highest rate of Indigenous persons with disability using disability support services, at close to 100 per cent of the potential disability population, while Tasmania has the lowest. Rates for Indigenous service use by potential population are higher than the non-Indigenous population in all States and Territories, except in Tasmania (Fig. 3.5).

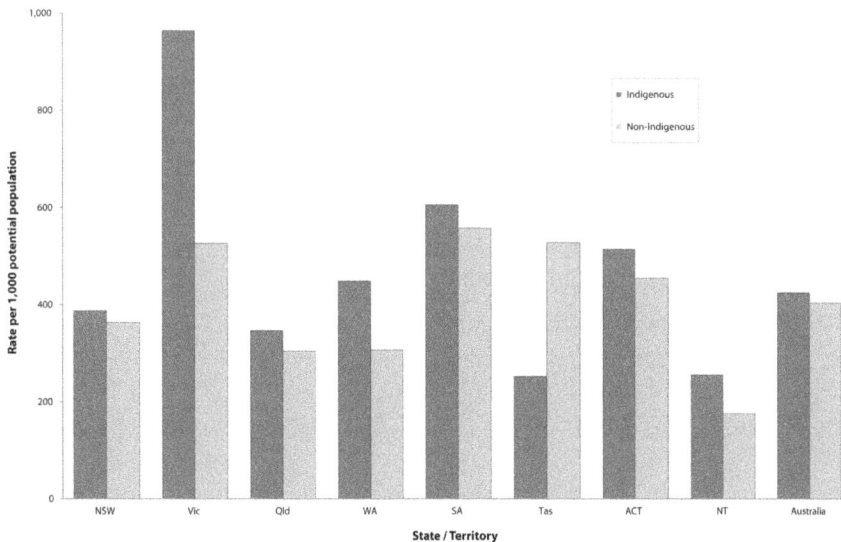

Fig. 3.5 Users of disability support services by Indigenous status and State/Territory, aged 0–64 years, Australia, 2009–10[a]

a. Service models vary across jurisdiction and may affect comparability of data.

Source: AIHW analysis of DS NMDS 2009–10; see Appendix Table A5.19

An increase in the proportion of Indigenous people with disability receiving services occurred in every State and Territory of Australia in the previous five years, except South Australia and the Northern Territory. A large increase was recorded in the Australian Capital Territory in 2009–10 (Fig. 3.6).

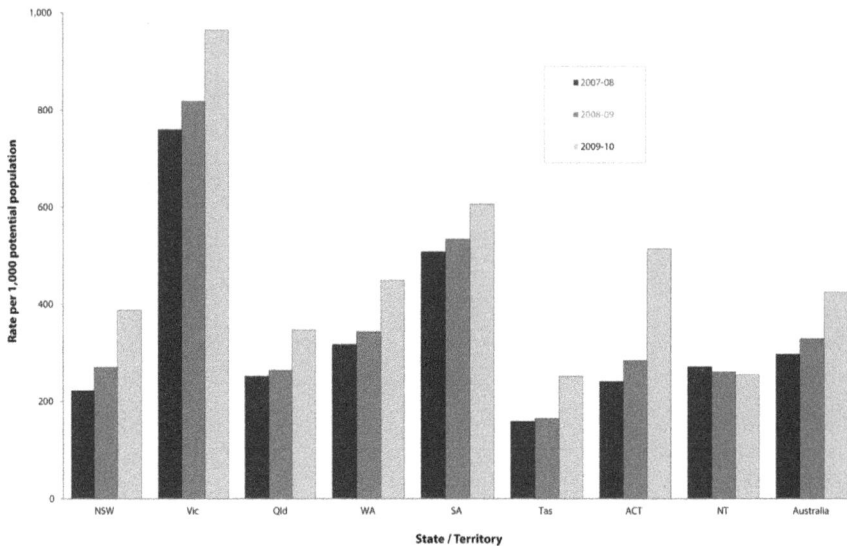

Fig. 3.6 Indigenous users of disability support services by State/Territory, aged 0–64 years, Australia, 2005–06 to 2009–10[a]

a. Service models vary across jurisdiction and may affect comparability of data.

Source: AIHW analysis of CSTDA NMDS 2007–08, 2008–09, DS NMDS 2009–10; see Appendix Table A5.19

The rate of service use for both Indigenous and non-Indigenous Australians with disability was highest for the 15–24 year age group (102% for Indigenous and 86% for non-Indigenous: note that rates of service use may exceed 100% where some users of services are not identified as having a severe or profound core activity limitation, or where errors have been made in the recording of Indigenous status or age). Service use was lowest among those aged 55–64 years (15% for Indigenous and 16% for non-Indigenous) (Table 3.4). As has been noted previously, while the service rate for Indigenous Australians is above that of non-Indigenous Australians this is driven by the result for the 15–24 age group, with all of the other age groups showing a lower service rate for the Indigenous population relative to need.

Table 3.4 Disability service use rates for persons aged 0–64 years, by age group and Indigenous status, Australia, 2009–10[a]

Age group	Indigenous Australians			Non-Indigenous Australians		
	Potential population[b]	Service users	Service rate (%)[c]	Potential population	Service users	Service rate (%)
0–4	1 992	1 065	53.5	29 779	18 290	61.4
5–14	8 364	2 471	29.5	125 215	32 281	25.8
15–24	3 471	3 526	101.6	53 462	45 718	85.5
25–34	3 029	2 027	66.9	58 535	39 320	67.2
35–44	4 743	2 164	45.6	82 751	41 451	50.1
45–54	5 885	1 691	28.7	120 836	43 361	35.9
55–64	6 081	929	15.3	182 991	29 173	15.9
Total (0–64)	33 566	13 873	41.3	653 569	249 594	38.2

a. The term 'Indigenous' refers to service users who identified as Aboriginal and/or Torres Strait Islander people. 'Non-Indigenous' refers to service users who reported not being of Aboriginal or Torres Strait Islander background.

b. Indigenous potential population estimates are experimental. Indigenous potential population estimates are calculated by applying Indigenous/non-Indigenous sex and 10-year age group rates of severe/profound disability in each State/Territory from the Survey of Disability and Carers (SDAC) 2003 to Indigenous and non-Indigenous population projection data for 2008 in each State/Territory by sex and 10-year age group for people aged 0–64. Indigenous population figures are based on ABS Series B projections of the Indigenous population by State/Territory for June 2008 (ABS 2009a).

c. Rates of service use may exceed 100% where some users of services are not identified as having a severe or profound core activity limitation, or where errors have been made in the recording of Indigenous status or age.

Source: AIHW analysis of NDA NMDS 2009–10 (AIHW 2011b); revised ABS Series B projections of the Indigenous population by State/Territory for June 2009 (ABS 2009a)

In 2009–10, access to disability support services by Indigenous persons with disability were lowest in major cities (285 per 1 000 population), and highest in outer regional/remote/very remote areas (626 per 1 000 population). The access rate has consistently increased in all remoteness areas over the last five years (Fig. 3.7).

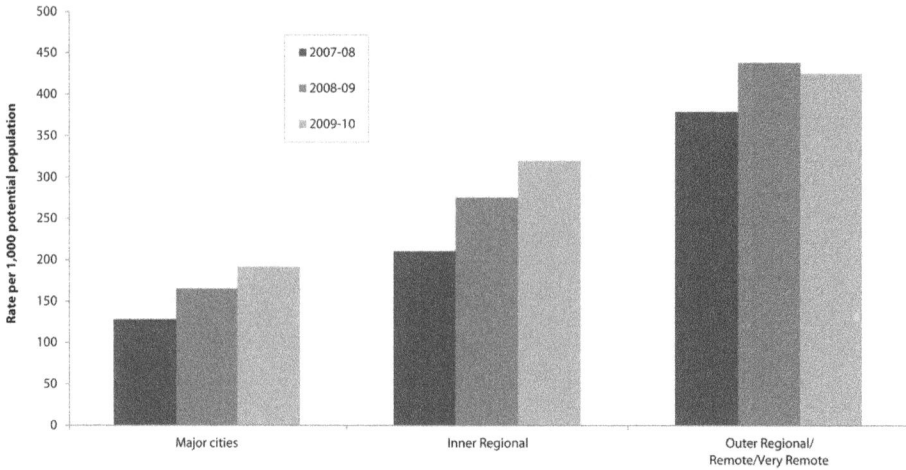

Fig. 3.7 Indigenous users of disability support services, by Indigenous status and remoteness, aged 0–64 years, Australia, 2005–06 to 2009–10ª

a. Service models vary across jurisdiction and may affect comparability of data.

Source: AIHW analysis of CSTDA NMDS 2007–08, 2008–09, DS NMDS 2009–10; see Appendix Table A5.20

Barriers to accessing services

This section examines the information available on the extent to which Indigenous persons with disability report problems accessing services, and if they do experience problems, the reasons for this and whether this varies according to geographic remoteness.

The 2008 NATSISS included a question concerning whether the respondent had problems accessing selected services for persons aged 15 years and over. Examples of services include doctors, dentists, hospitals, employment services, Centrelink, banks and other financial institutions, Medicare, mental health services and other services. While the GSS lists disability services as a separate category, the NATSISS does not (disability services is likely to fall under the category 'other services'). Respondents were also asked about types of barriers to accessing services such as transport/distance and cost.

The 2008 NATSISS found that nearly half of Indigenous Australians with severe or profound core activity limitations identified having problems accessing service providers (Table 3.5). The 2006 GSS found that almost half of all Australians with severe or profound disability were experiencing problems accessing services (Table 3.6).

Table 3.5 Problems accessing service providers, Indigenous Australians aged 18–64 years, by disability, Australia, 2008[a]

	People with severe or profound core activity limitations (%)	People with no disability or long-term health condition (%)
Had problems	46	27
Did not have problems	54	73
Total (no.)	20 722	135 441

a. 2008 NATSISS included remote, very remote and indigenous communities, but excluded special dwellings where higher proportions of people with severe and profound disability may be located.

Source: AIHW 2011b: Table A9

Table 3.6 Problems accessing service providers, all Australians aged 18–64 years, by disability, 2006[a]

	People with severe or profound core activity limitations (%)	People with no disability or long-term health condition (%)
Had problems	46	27
Did not have problems	54	73
Total (no.)	20 722	135 441

a. 2006 GSS excluded very remote and sparsely settled areas and excluded special dwellings where higher proportions of people with severe or profound disability may be found.

Source: AIHW 2011b: Table A10

Table 3.7 shows that the proportion of Indigenous people who had problems accessing services varied by age group and disability status. Those aged 25–34 years and 35–44 years were most likely to experience problems accessing services, regardless of their disability status. However 'problems accessing services' was more commonly reported by persons aged 15–24 years with a profound or severe core activity limitation than by persons of the same age with any type of disability, or no disability or long-term health condition (more than 50%).

Table 3.7 Problems accessing services, Indigenous persons aged 15 years and over, by age group, Australia, 2008[a]

	Age group					
	15–24	25–34	35–44	45–54	55 +	Total
Has profound or severe core-activity limitation						
Had problems accessing services	44.9	50.2	52.7	44.2	35.0	43.8
Did not have problems accessing services	55.1	49.8	47.3	55.8	65.0	56.2
Total	100.0	100.0	100.0	100.0	100.0	100.0
Total with disability or long-term health condition						
Had problems accessing services	30.8	41.1	40.2	36.5	31.4	35.8
Did not have problems accessing services	69.2	58.9	59.8	63.5	68.6	64.2
Total	100.0	100.0	100.0	100.0	100.0	100.0
Has no disability or long-term health condition						
Had problems accessing services	18.3	28.6	29.0	26.9	26.0	24.1
Did not have problems accessing services	81.7	71.4	71.0	73.1	74.0	75.9
Total	100.0	100.0	100.0	100.0	100.0	100.0

a. 2008 NATSISS included remote, very remote and indigenous communities but excluded special dwellings where higher proportions of people with severe and profound disability may be found.

Source: AIHW analysis of ABS 2008 NATSISS (unpublished)

Information on the extent to which Indigenous people report a range of barriers to accessing services is provided in Fig. 3.8. It demonstrates how this varies according to geographic remoteness and whether a person has a severe or profound core activity limitation (labelled as a 'disability' in Fig. 3.8).

In remote areas, the barriers to accessing services most commonly reported by those with disability are 'no services in the area' (25%) or 'not enough services in the area' (24%), transport/distance (21%), and 'waiting time too long or not available at time required' (20%). These barriers to accessing services were also the most commonly reported by people without disability (Fig. 3.9). In non-remote areas, waiting time too long (18%) and cost of service (12%) were the most commonly reported barrier to accessing services by Indigenous people with disability. Indigenous persons with disability or long-term health condition were twice as likely to report services as not being culturally appropriate and discrimination as barriers to accessing services, as Indigenous persons without disability: 3 per cent compared to 1.5 per cent for services not culturally appropriate and 1.9 per cent compared to 0.7 per cent for treated badly/discrimination.

The 2004–05 National Aboriginal and Torres Strait Islander Health Survey (NATSIHS) collected data on whether Indigenous persons needed to access particular health services (dentists, doctors, other health professionals, hospitals) and did not do so in the last 12 months, and the reasons for not accessing these services when needed. Similar to data collected for the NATSISS, the most common service Indigenous people needed to access but did not was a dentist. The most common reasons for not accessing a dental service was cost and waiting time or service not available at time of request.

The most common reasons reported by Indigenous Australians for not accessing a doctor or other health professional were being too busy with work; personal or family responsibilities; and cost. A large proportion of Indigenous people who did not access a hospital when needed reported reasons related to dislike for the service or professional, and being afraid or embarrassed (see Appendix Table A5.22).

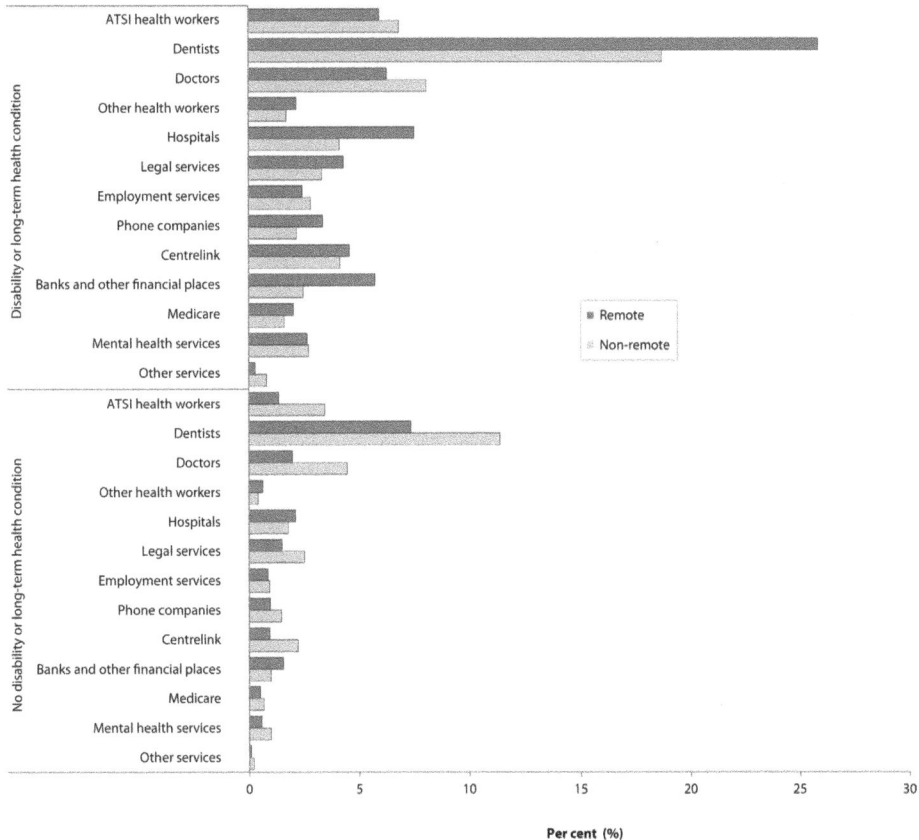

Fig. 3.8 Type of barrier to access service, Indigenous persons aged 15 years and over, by presence of a disability and remoteness, Australia, 2008

Source: AIHW analysis of 2008 NATSISS; see Appendix Table A5.22

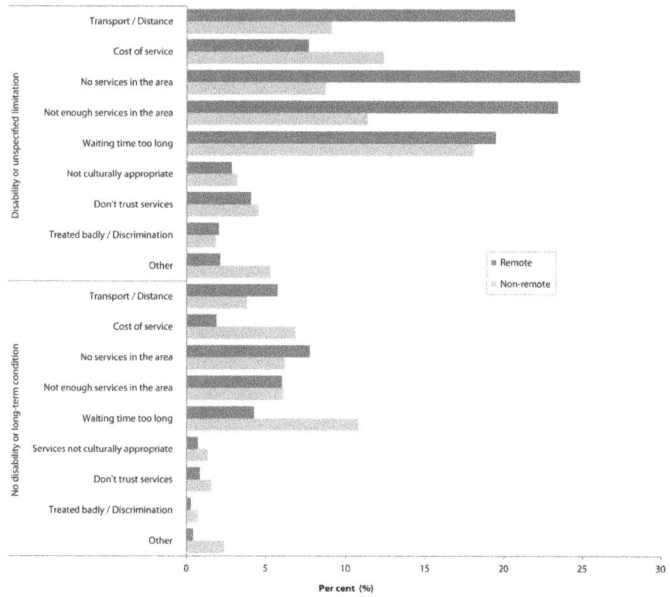

Fig. 3.9 Access problem to type of service, Indigenous persons aged 15 years and over, by presence of a disability and remoteness, Australia, 2008

Source: NATSISS 2008: see Appendix Table A5.21

4. Current dataset gaps and limitations

As has been seen in analysis thus far, a range of different data sets have had to be drawn upon to try to identify the level and incidence of disability amongst Indigenous people, and their level of access to support services. In discussion a number of weaknesses have been identified in the data. These are considered in more detail in this chapter.

There are a number of gaps and limitations in current data collections on disability including:

- under-identification of Indigenous Australians in administrative data and population surveys

- gaps in coverage in survey data e.g. age groups, remoteness status

- limitations on the degree to which survey data that is collected on Indigenous Australians with disability is comparable to data collected on either non-Indigenous people or all people with disability.

Apart from differences in the data items collected between various groups, there are a number of issues specific to Indigenous Australians with disability. These include problems with the cultural appropriateness of the survey instrument content, whether the data that are being collected accurately measure the concept of disability, and culturally appropriate administration of the survey instrument. Indigenous-specific surveys such as the NATSISS are less prone than mainstream surveys and collections to such complexities as they usually involve consultations with Indigenous communities and pilot testing of questions with Indigenous persons to ensure they are culturally appropriate.

A further challenge in estimating the extent and nature of disability in the Indigenous population is that, as mentioned above, self-reported measures of disability are likely to underestimate the extent of the Indigenous population affected by disability. According to the FPDN submission to the Productivity Commission (FPDN 2011: 3), there is a 'reluctance of Aboriginal and Torres Strait Islander people with disabilities to identify as people with disability'.

Historically much of the focus on Aboriginal and Torres Strait Islander people with disability has been from a health perspective. Whilst this is essential, it fails to recognise the social aspects of Aboriginal and Torres Strait Islander disability. Furthermore, the impact of colonisation and the resultant dispossession of land have had an impact on the lives of many Indigenous people with disability, and this is very difficult to measure as part of a survey instrument. The reasons many Indigenous people may not identify as having a disability include:

- not wishing to take on another negative label when Indigenous Australians already experience discrimination based on their Aboriginality

- no comparable word to disability existing in some traditional Aboriginal languages, suggesting that disability may have been accepted as part of the human experience

- disability being viewed as a consequence of having 'married the wrong way' in some communities that continue to practice a more traditional lifestyle: those with disability and their family members may experience stigma related to negative social conceptions of disability, and

- a medical model of disability, often focusing heavily on primary health interventions, which has had a profoundly negative impact on the lives of many Aboriginal and Torres Strait Islander people with disability. In particular, the model does not address the whole of life needs of Aboriginal and Torres Strait Islander people with disability.

These issues have been raised earlier in this volume. However, it is worth reiterating that these factors also have an effect on data collections. Surveys tend to assume a shared perception of concepts such as 'disability', 'caring', and 'need for assistance'. Indigenous perceptions of these concepts may be different to the assumptions upon which statistical surveys are based (Aboriginal Disability Network New South Wales 2007; Helps and Moller 2007: 44–6; NSW Ombudsman 2010; House of Representatives Standing Committee on Family, Housing and Youth Affairs 2009; Senior 2000; Stopher and D'Antoine 2008). Unless carefully developed in the context of Indigenous understandings and experience, efforts to measure and quantify disability among the Aboriginal and Torres Strait Islander population is difficult.

Census and survey data on disability prevalence

Census of Population and Housing

The Census of Population and Housing is conducted by the ABS at five-yearly intervals, with 2011 being the most recent. As noted above, the 2011 Census data became available after the analysis for this report was completed, and while some limited 2011 Census data has been included, the majority of the census data reported here is from the 2006 Census.

A measure of disability was developed for the 2006 Census, conceptually similar to SDAC but telescoped into four questions for practical administration within a national census. These questions identified those people with a 'need for assistance' in one of the core activities of self-care, communication or mobility, similar to those identified as having severe or profound core activity limitations in SDAC. However, the census requires a representative of the individual household to complete a form. Ascertainment of Indigenous status tends to be lower in self-report forms (ABS 2007; Steering Committee for the Review of Government Service Provision (SCRGSP) 2009) and the non-response rate on the 'need for assistance' questions among those who do identify as Indigenous was 7 per cent in 2006, compared with 2 per cent for non-Indigenous people (ABS and AIHW 2008). Hence, under-representation of Indigenous people with disability may have occurred. The census form may be completed by one household member on behalf of others. Incorrect answers can be introduced to the census form if the respondent does not understand the question or does not know the correct information about other household members.

Survey of Disability and Carers

The SDAC is the most comprehensive survey conducted by the ABS that provides data on disability at the population level. It collects information about a wide range of impairments, activity limitations and participation restrictions, and their effects on the everyday lives of people with disability, older people and their carers. This survey has the advantage of covering special dwellings, such as cared accommodation, as well as non-private and private dwellings. The most recent data available are for 2009, which for the first time collected information on Indigenous status, although the sample size was too small for any findings for Indigenous Australians to be released publicly. Also, the SDAC does not collect data in very remote areas and is therefore limited in comparisons that can be undertaken between Indigenous and non-Indigenous people (ABS 2010a).

National Aboriginal and Torres Strait Islander Social Survey

The 2008 NATSISS collected information by personal interview from 13 300 Indigenous Australians across all States and Territories of Australia, including those living in remote areas. The sample covered persons aged 15 years and over who are usual residents in selected private dwellings. The NATSISS is conducted every six years, with the next survey in the field at the time of publication.

The NATSISS includes a short Disability Module, based on the SDAC. It identifies those with disability and the 'severity of disability' experience. However, it does not include people who live in special dwellings, such as institutions, group homes and hostels, where people with more severe disability are often located.

The 2008 NATSISS has a relatively large level of undercoverage when compared to other ABS surveys. That is, a large proportion of the Indigenous population are missed in selecting the sample. There was also an increase in undercoverage compared to previous ABS Indigenous surveys. For example, the estimated undercoverage in the 2004–05 NATSIHS was 42 per cent. The overall under-coverage rate for the 2008 NATSISS is approximately 53 per cent of the in-scope population at the national level. This rate varies across the States and Territories (ABS 2010b). Further information on NATSISS data quality issues can be found in the 2008 NATSISS *User's Guide* (ABS 2010b).

Administrative data on disability services

Disability Services National Minimum Data Set

The DS NMDS (formerly Commonwealth State/Territory Disability Agreement NMDS as described in Chapter 3) provides data only on people receiving services and hence these data can address neither the characteristics, nor the service and support needs of people not receiving services.

The collection does not include all disability support services in Australia: it includes only those where funding has been provided for the specified period by a government organisation operating under the NDA. The scope of services included in the DS NMDS therefore varies in terms of programs that receive funding across jurisdictions. For example, in 2009–10 in Victoria and Queensland, specialist psychiatric disability services were provided under the NDA. However, in all other jurisdictions specific mental health services were funded and provided under health, rather than disability, portfolios and were therefore not included in the DS NMDS. This is likely to explain some of the differences by State/Territory in 'met need' presented in Fig. 3.5.

Indigenous status information was missing/not stated for approximately 5 per cent of clients in the DS NMDS for the latest year of data available (2009–10) when this analysis was undertaken. This varied by State/Territory from 0.3 per cent in South Australia to 11.2 per cent in Victoria. Rates of missing/not stated Indigenous status have fallen markedly over the past five years from around 10 per cent in 2005–06. It should also be noted that agencies providing recreation and holiday programs are not required to collect information on clients' Indigenous status. Although this is not considered to be 'missing/unknown/not stated' data, these programs/services contribute to the incomplete representation of the number of Indigenous people who receive disability support services in Australia.

The presence of 'not stated' Indigenous status data is an indication that identification of Indigenous people accessing the disability support services is incomplete. It is not known what proportion of clients with 'not stated' Indigenous status are of Aboriginal or Torres Strait Islander origin, or what proportion of Indigenous clients are incorrectly recorded as non-Indigenous. 'Not stated' Indigenous status data may occur due to a number of reasons. Staff members who collect data may hold negative attitudes, lack training, or have other reasons for hesitating to ask the Indigenous status question, for instance, due to concerns about provoking aggressive responses from both Indigenous and non-Indigenous clients. Staff members might make assumptions about a client's Indigenous status based upon their appearance, and therefore fail to ask the question. Finally, clients may be concerned about the differential treatment of Indigenous clients and refuse to answer the question.

The willingness of clients to identify as Indigenous may be influenced by a number of factors related to the type of the service provided, including the purpose of the service and the voluntary nature of the clients' access to the service. For instance, clients of disability support services make voluntary contact with the service, and a sense of social stigma surrounding their situation may impede clients' readiness to identify as Indigenous.

A summary table of current data sources on disability for the Indigenous population, data items of relevance to the NDIS and data quality/data gaps is available from the website for this volume in Appendix 4 Table A4.1. A summary of key questions from the data sources that will help to inform the NDIS for Indigenous persons and mapping to available data is available in Appendix 3 Table A3.1.

Other community service data collections which include an Indigenous identifier

Community service data collections (other than the DS NMDS) which contain disability-related data items are outlined in Table 4.1.

Table 4.1 Community service data collections: Scope, related data and data quality

Data collection	Scope/ population	Disability related data items	Data quality
Home and Community Age Care (HACC)	Clients accessing the HACC program which provides funding for services supporting people who live at home with decreased capacity for independent living, or who are at risk of premature or inappropriate admission to long-term residential care.	Level of functioning (functional status) up to 14 activity areas	Functional status data is poor quality—WA is the only State to collect this data for high proportion of clients (93%). There are differing requirements for collection of this data in different States.
Community Aged Care Packages (CACP)	Recipients of CACPs which target those with 'low-care' needs	Need for assistance with core activities and non-core activities by type	Need for assistance information is not a standard part of this collection—the latest available was collected from the 2008 Community Care Census, for which data by Indigenous status is not available. CACP collection does not collect data from the flexible community aged care places operating under the Aboriginal and Torres Strait Islander Aged Care Strategy or operational flexible community care places provided by Multi-Purpose Services. This, as well as the fact that responses to the Indigenous status question are not mandatory may contribute to an under-representation of the number and proportion of Indigenous clients in this data collection.
Younger People with Disability in Residential Aged Care (YPIRAC)	Younger people with disability living in residential aged care. While the initial priority of the YPIRAC initiative targets people with disability aged under 50, where possible, people with disability under the age of 65 are also targeted.	Primary disability group Other significant disability group(s)	Most data items are very well reported. In 2008–09, data were provided for all service users for the linkage key items (name, date of birth and sex), residential setting, Indigenous status, primary disability group and postcode. The largest proportion of 'not stated' responses was the principal reason for the service user's current accommodation setting, at 7.5%.
National Child Protection (NCP) Data Collection	All children and young people involved in the child protection systems throughout Australia	Need for assistance with activities in life area (ICF) Disability group	Need for assistance data has not been published from this collection to date due to quality issues. Unit record level data not currently available (therefore data not available by remoteness or lower-level geography). However, a unit-record collection is scheduled to be implemented in mid 2013.

Source: Author's analysis

Current plans for improving disability data

Disability Services data

The NDA came into effect on 1 January 2009, and called for jurisdictions to work on 'improvements in the quality of data reported under the National Minimum Data Set'. A few reported activities specifically address Indigenous identification such as the implementation of the standard Indigenous status question. Jurisdictions currently vary in their practices to collect and record Indigenous status data. Not all disability services in all jurisdictions are using the standard Indigenous status question, response options or recording categories. However, steps are being taken to ensure consistency among service providers in different jurisdictions.

The AIHW is currently working on redevelopment of the DS NMDS to enhance the content and quality of information that is currently collected about all clients, including Indigenous clients, and to provide a better picture of the needs of people with a disability by collecting information about their needs for assistance, the support they require, and the outcomes of the services they receive. Additional data elements that are proposed for inclusion in the DS NMDS are anticipated to provide better quality information about geographical location, including Remoteness Area and a State/Territory identifier. Data elements about carers (where they live, age, sex, and their relationship to the person with disability) and data elements about living arrangements, labour force status, and main source of income are also proposed.

The DS NMDS redevelopment aims to support the development and implementation of the NDIS. The redevelopment will ensure that the DS NMDS can provide the data standards required to underpin the administrative and technical systems of the NDIS in areas such as the quantification of services and the measurement of client outcomes. In addition it will seek to align the collection with the Home and Community Aged Care (HACC) and Younger People with Disability in Residential Aged Care (YPIRAC) collections and considering how the data development will support person-centred care and the NDIS.

Disability module included in ABS surveys

Work is underway to modify the Disability Module so that results for the identification of the population with disability more closely correspond to those in the SDAC. This work will require extensive consultation with stakeholders and testing of the revised module. Once a revised module is implemented, the ABS will test the results for quality and comparability with the SDAC.

Standard Disability identifier in community services collections

The AIHW is currently undertaking work to develop a recommended standard set of disability data elements for use in community services (and potentially housing) data collections. The AIHW is currently consulting on a suite of items for inclusion. Wide consultation involving support workers, policy makers, and data providers in each sector will be essential prior to any pilot test.

Addressing data gaps/improved methods of data collection

The following recommendations are made to help to address some of the data gaps and limitations outlined above.

Recommendation 1

The Disability Module included in the NATSISS and GSS should be modified to reflect the SDAC more closely in future surveys. This would involve ABS work already underway, outlined above, which will ensure that the results for the disability population correspond with those in the SDAC. It would also include an assessment of which data items included in the SDAC and not currently included in the NATSISS/GSS would provide useful information for the Indigenous population. Cost-benefit analyses would then need to be undertaken to determine whether they could be added to future NATSISS/GSS surveys.

Recommendation 2

If the above is not feasible, then the sample size for Indigenous Australians in the SDAC could be increased to enable reliable estimates for the Indigenous population at State/Territory and remoteness levels. This should be considered regardless of whether Recommendation 1 is feasible, as there are advantages to collecting detailed information on Indigenous and non-Indigenous people in the one survey.

Recommendation 3

In terms of data analysis, when analysing core activity need for assistance data from the 2006 Census, non-response (not stated) responses to the disability status questions should be excluded, as they are particularly high compared to the other surveys e.g. NATSISS/GSS. This should also be kept in mind if this high level of non-response is replicated in the 2011 and future censuses.

Recommendation 4

Indigenous status is also under-identified in the census. Ideally, conclusions based on the census should derive from population estimates rather than population counts. Furthermore, additional work ought to be undertaken to examine methods to assess the level of Indigenous under-identification in DS NMDS data in order to gain a better understanding of the level of under-identification in this collection, as it is currently not known.

Recommendation 5

Future NATSISS surveys should collect disability information for persons of all ages—that is, collect from persons under the age of 15 years. Future surveys should consider expanding the broader criteria to remote areas to address gaps in coverage.

Recommendation 6

For future NATSISS surveys, 'Disability services' should be added as a specific category to the data item on types of services people have problems accessing. This will provide comparable data on the Indigenous population to that obtained for the general population from the GSS. In addition, it is also worth considering some questions on the extent to which service needs are being met, and not only problems of access.

Recommendation 7

The final recommendation with regard to data collection is for further research work to develop measures of disability that are more conceptually relevant to measuring this concept in the Indigenous population, looking at patterns of impairment and also the impact of impairment within the contexts in which Indigenous people live. This is not merely a data issue as it will involve a mixture of quantitative data collection and analysis, qualitative research, and case studies. Ideally, this research should focus not only on individuals and their families, but also service providers. Given the money to be invested in the NDIS, this would appear to be an important component of the process of ensuring that the scheme secures the maximum benefit for Indigenous Australians.

5. Delivering disability services

Although the majority of Indigenous Australians live in major cities and inner regional areas, a much higher proportion of the Indigenous population resides in outer regional, remote and very remote areas than is the case for the non-Indigenous population. While a number of the issues that need to be considered when delivering disability services to Indigenous Australians apply in all geographic areas, there is a set of specific issues that relates to providing services in regional, remote and very remote areas. This chapter discusses key issues involved in delivering disability services to Indigenous people and possible delivery models. Several possible models and approaches to service delivery are discussed and, drawing upon the existing evidence base, where it exists, the advantages and disadvantages of different models are outlined.

Implications of the nature of Indigenous disability for service delivery

While there are many similarities in the nature of disability experienced by Indigenous and non-Indigenous Australians, there are some distinctive aspects of disability in the Indigenous population which have important implications for the delivery of services. Key features of disability in the Indigenous population are:

- a significantly higher rate of disability in the Indigenous population, especially after adjusting for age

- impairment tends to occurs in earlier age groups for the Indigenous population

- Indigenous people with a disability are relatively more likely to have an intellectual disability than are non-Indigenous people with a disability

- there is a higher incidence of complex needs and issues which span health, disability and other issues; an example is substance abuse combined with cognitive impairment[1]

- many Indigenous people with a disability are themselves caring for one or more other persons with a disability[2]

---

1 Wilkes et al. (2010) report that Indigenous men are over four times, and Indigenous women over three times, more likely to be hospitalised for mental disorders attributable to psychoactive substance misuse than their non-Indigenous counterparts.
2 According to the 2008 NATSISS, about half of Indigenous people with a disability were caring for somebody else with a disability.

- cultural differences in perceptions of disability and of identification as having a disability amongst some groups of Indigenous Australians.

There are also a number of interactions between these factors. For example, when combined with substance abuse, intellectual disabilities are often associated with behaviours that are challenging from a service provider perspective. Furthermore, the impact of disability on a person's ability to function is determined by the interaction between the physical nature of their disability and the physical, economic and social environment within which they live. There are clear differences between the environment in which the Indigenous population with a disability live and that of the non-Indigenous population and these can have important implications for the impact of disability on people's lives as well as the nature of service needs.

One set of differences relate to geographic remoteness. Some of the implications for services arising from geographic remoteness are:

- low population density, which can provide a number of challenges to service delivery, making it more expensive than in cities and larger towns

- difficulties in attracting and retaining a professional skilled workforce

- distance from key infrastructure, such as hospitals

- often a lack of physical infrastructure or poor-quality infrastructure e.g. roads, suitable buildings

- harsh climatic conditions and inaccessibility due to weather events for extended periods of time.

Writing about a Northern Territory community, Senior (2000: 10) notes:

> The physical environment of the community is limiting to people with disabilities. The roads are dirt and deeply corrugated causing great difficulties for those in wheelchairs or who are unsteady on their feet. In the wet season the roads are often flooded and always boggy. Moving around the community can be very difficult. Transport is also a problem for members of the community. Very few people have cars and public transport is limited.

There are a range of factors that need to be taken into account when delivering services to Indigenous Australians. As there is a great deal of diversity within the Indigenous community, the following issues will apply to a differing extent to particular individuals, groups or communities.

- The nature of family, family networks, and the ways in which informal care is provided.

- Mistrust of government services arising from negative past experiences, or simply an individual's feeling that government services are not for them.

- Higher rates of low income and economic deprivation.

- Relatively low levels of education and associated low levels of literacy and numeracy. In some communities, English is not the first language spoken.

- Cultural differences in the way in which disability is perceived, understood and responded to, and the ways in which it impacts on people's lives.[3]

- Being over-represented in the criminal and juvenile justice systems, and in the care and protection system, both as parents and children.

Current disability service delivery models and systems in States and Territories

A variety of disability service delivery models are currently operating in Australia.[4] The key features of the system in each State and Territory in 2012 are summarised here and in Fisher et al. (2010). There are differences in the extent of individual support packages (ISPs) and consumer control over how their support package is allocated. Nonetheless, there appears to be a trend towards individualised funding models with some jurisdictions having had individualised funding models and consumers having had much more say in the services they access for a significant period of time (in the case of Western Australia since 1988), while others are trialling ISPs and consumer choice (e.g. South Australia).

---

3   However, as noted earlier, there is relatively little qualitative research on this issue and very little if any quantitative research.
4   As part of the National Disability Agreement (NDA), the Commonwealth, State and Territory governments have agreed that a priority is to increase the access of Indigenous Australians to disability services. The National Disability Agreement National Indigenous Access Framework has been agreed to by Commonwealth, State and Territory governments. The framework is available from http://www.dprwg.gov.au/research-development/publications/national-indigenous-access-framework (accessed 27 November 2012).

Disability service models operating in Australia

New South Wales

The funding model in New South Wales is for a wide range of community support and specialist care provided directly by Ageing, Disability and Home Care (ADHC) or through the Home Care Service of New South Wales, a statutory authority. ADHC also funds 900 local governments and non-government organisations (NGOs) to provide services.

In terms of the degree of individual control, New South Wales is in the formative stages of self-directed support. Some pilots with small numbers of people include:

- The Attendant Care Program – direct payment model
- Community Participation – self managed model
- Family Assistance Fund
- My Plan, My Choice – Early Start
- My Plan, My Choice – Older Carers program
- Life Choices and Active Ageing – self-managed model
- Extended family support
- Younger People in Residential Aged Care (YPIRAC) Program

Intermediaries are commonly used. ADHC currently offers two models of individual funding: the first where a portable funding package is held by the service provider, which provides or buys disability support for the person; the second involves the person or family receiving a direct payment to purchase disability support from the open market, including service providers.

An Indigenous specific program called Services Our Way (SOW) is a demonstration project commenced in 2010–11. It is available to Aboriginal people (in the trial area) with a diagnosed intellectual or physical disability, including Acquired Brain Injury and Multiple Sclerosis. SOW is based on an ISP with the funds held by the agency. The program is delivered by Aboriginal Support Specialists. It should also be noted that an ADHC Aboriginal Advisory Committee was established in June 2011.

As far as rural/remote specific programs are concerned, the rural and remote working group was formed in 2010. Remote videoconferencing facilities have been developed.

Victoria

The funding model in Victoria is a mix of ISPs (to service provider or financial intermediary or through a direct payment) and block funding through the Community Sector Investment Fund. The Department of Human Services offers specialist disability services including short-term supports (such as respite services, behaviour supports, case management and therapy), and ongoing supports (such as ISPs and shared supported accommodation). It should be noted that the demand for ISPs exceeds supply. A report on the effectiveness of individualised funding has been published (Victorian Auditor-General's Office 2011).

The degree of individual control is indicated by the *Victorian State Disability Plan 2002–12* which emphasises individual needs and choices (since the time of this research, the *Victorian State Disability Plan 2013–16* has been released). In 2010–11, around 700–800 people had an ISP, receiving 19 per cent of annual total disability funding. People on an ISP can use any combination of direct payments, a financial intermediary service, and/or a registered disability service provider. ISPs are approved regionally, but once obtained, funding can be moved to another region. If the participant moves interstate, funding moves with them for a 12 month period. Participants can buy services delivered just to them or buy group-based services. Facilitators are available to help people to develop a personal plan for their needs and goals, and a funding proposal, but the person with disability or a supporter may take on this role if they wish. The regional office assesses the funding proposal, which must be reviewed at least every three years. Funding cannot be used to employ staff directly, unless as part of the Direct Employment Project Trial and with departmental approval, or employed by a service provider. Family members (not living in same dwelling) may be employed if they meet these criteria.

The Indigenous specific programs operating in Victoria are the Closing the Gap project, and the Disability Services Cultural and Linguistic Diversity Strategy.

Queensland

Funding for disability services in Queensland is a mix of block funding, targeted funding, individual funding, and hybrid funding models. Specialist disability services are delivered by Disability Services Queensland and the non-government service providers funded by it. The Growing Stronger program of reform (2007–11) aimed to build a better specialist disability service system, shifting from an input-funding focus to funding for output-based service provision

(Disability Services Queensland 2007). In July 2011, program structures (Post School Services, Family Support Program and Adult Lifestyle Support Program) were discontinued in favour of individualised assessments of needs.

The degree of individual control is limited in Queensland as block funding is the central approach. Some service providers do offer people control over their funding; however if a person receives funding directly, they must incorporate as an organisation and meet the requirements of a service provider. A small-scale program—the Self-Directed Support Pilot Program—involved 80 people over two years, and was directed at people without existing links to the community and without prior funding from Disability Services Queensland.

In terms of Indigenous specific programs there is an interpreter and translation assistance strategy. As far as rural/remote specific programs is concerned, Local Area Coordinators in rural and remote communities are employed to focus on strengthening individuals and communities with an emphasis on building natural and local supports.

South Australia

The funding model for South Australia is centred on Disability Services as the government service provider for people with disabilities. It provides supported accommodation, service coordination and specialist services. Services are also provided by non-government service providers. Individual funding is based on portable funding held by a service provider. While individual funding packages are common, they are not available across all service types.

The degree of personalisation is limited to a new approach to individualised funding, with a trial of 50 people that commenced in June 2010. Each participant was provided with a 'self-management facilitator', to help participants and their support network develop a personal plan. The participant (or proxy) may arrange and purchase services, decide what to buy but pay an organisation to manage the financial arrangements, or pay an organisation to arrange services and manage funds. The participant is helped in managing their funding through training, resource materials, an enquiry service, and their facilitator. Services must be purchased from organisations registered on the Disability Services Provider Panel, and participants must account for any use of funds, with quarterly and annual acquittals of the funding (and keep records of support and expenditure plans, receipts, invoices and relevant bank statements for seven years), with unspent money returned to the Department of Families and Communities after 12 months.

There is an Indigenous specific program through the Disability Services team of Aboriginal staff providing support for Aboriginal people with disability, their families and carers. They provide Aboriginal workers if preferred, assist in finding and using disability services, and provide advocacy and help clients to secure support. In addition, there is a Cultural Inclusion Team that provides leadership on policy, community consultation, and regional planning for disability services to Aboriginal and Torres Strait Islander people with disability, their families and communities. This includes researching needs, trends and priorities; developing policy within the department and other government sectors; and improving contract outcomes with non-government service provision.

In terms of rural/remote specific programs, the Independent Living Centre's Mobile Unit Outreach Service is a free government service for people living in rural and remote South Australia.

Western Australia

Under the Western Australia funding model, individualised funding has been progressively implemented since 1988 and applies to all recipients of State government disability funding since 2005. The full range of individual funding approaches is applied, with portable funds held by providers, facilitators and direct funding to individuals and families. Block funding is rarely used to fund service providers. Direct funding is facilitated through the Local Area Coordination Program, with a network of Local Area Coordinators assisting individuals to plan, select and receive services. Applications for individualised funding go through a Combined Application Process, which prioritises and allocates funding. A significant proportion of services are provided by NGOs.

There is a high degree of consumer control in Western Australia compared to other States under shared management with coordination, administrative and financial functions undertaken by the intermediary organisation (including helping recruit, train and supervise the carer, and all the tasks associated with service delivery, including designing the support package). The Local Area Coordination Program also includes a capacity for self-directed funding through untied funding to cover low-cost, one-off, critical urgent needs (with a 16% uptake).

There is an Indigenous specific package, Getting Services Right, for Aboriginal people and their families in Western Australia, and an Aboriginal project officer within National Disability Services and within the Disabilities Services Commission policy branch. Regarding rural/remote specific programs, the Disabilities Services Commission has a country resource and consultancy team; and the Country Services Coordination Directorate has a remote area strategy.

Tasmania

The Tasmania funding model involves disability services primarily delivered by NGOs, with the government retaining the role of funder and regulator. To access services in Tasmania, clients are assessed and referred by Gateway Services who provide local area support. Self-directed support in Tasmania is delivered principally through ISPs, where funds are portable and held by a service provider. Under the ISP, the person with a disability applies for a number of support hours up to 34 hours per week to receive personal care and respite assistance. The hours are allocated to the person and the funding contract is made with the non-government service provider. The Tasmanian Government does not directly fund the person: it enters into a three-way contract with both the person and the service provider. People may cash out their allocation (based on funds equivalent to the weekly allocation of hours) to purchase personal support while on holiday and to buy authorised respite services. There is some trialling of direct funding through intermediary service providers. The Tasmanian Government has indicated that it plans to increase the use of self-directed support following a KPMG review of disability services in 2008 (KPMG 2009).

Northern Territory

The Northern Territory funding model is undergoing major reform. Most disability services are provided through block funding to service providers, and ISPs are only used if block-funded services not available. The NGO sector is the major provider of services but is not reaching remote areas. In terms of individual control, at the time of the KPMG review of disability services (KPMG 2009), only around 10 per cent of funding was allocated to people through Individual Community Support Packages (ICSPs) based on individual assessments. The main role of ICSPs was to 'fill gaps in the Northern Territory Disability Service system with small and tailored packages'. ICSPs include the capacity for direct funding, paid and acquitted quarterly, and overseen by Disability Case Coordinators and Case Managers (with arrangements through Local Area Coordination now abandoned). The client has administrative responsibility for purchasing, managing expenditure, and accounting; they have substantial flexibility in purchasing from mainstream providers and from friends and neighbours as carers. Direct payments account for less than half of ICSPs.

Australian Capital Territory

In the Australian Capital Territory people with disability are required to register their interest to receive services or to change the type or level of services they receive. Funding is allocated through ISPs, allowing individuals to choose the type of service and support they receive; however block funding of service providers remains important. While an agreed total level of funding is allocated to an agency for a specific individual, the service agency pools the funds with block funds and may allocate them to other individuals.

In terms of individual control, there is a small level of self-directed support through ISPs which are based on individual assessment, and generally occur through a service provider. This can take the form of individually tiered funding (brokered funding), individualised funding (direct funding), and individual grants (small non-recurrent allocations for a specific period, but with considerable flexibility about how they are acquitted). Local area coordination is provided through two community sector sites, rather than by government.

Indigenous specific programs are provided through several avenues. Aboriginal and Torres Strait Islander Services is part of the Office for Children, Youth and Family Support and aims to provide culturally appropriate services. Carers ACT Indigenous Carer Program provides assistance on request for counselling, information and advice, service referrals, case management, social support in general, and education and training. Disability ACT is developing a Draft Policy Framework for Aboriginal and Torres Strait Islander People with a Disability and Their Families (Disability ACT 2011).

The context of service delivery

Remote communities

It is widely recognised that a lack of access to services and infrastructure are important contributors to the high levels of disadvantage experienced in many remote Indigenous communities. The situation is clearly described in a recent Council of Australian Governments (COAG) report as a mixture of patchy service delivery, ad hoc and short-term programs, poor coordination, and confusion over roles and responsibilities. Complications have been exacerbated by Indigenous specific programs being added, often to replace missing mainstream services and/or without any relationship to community development priorities (COAG 2008).

Services in remote Indigenous communities are jointly funded by State and Territory governments and the Commonwealth Government and are often delivered by NGOs. Over the period 1990–2004, Commonwealth funding was provided to Indigenous community organisations largely via the Aboriginal and Torres Strait Islander Commission (ATSIC) and subsequently by Aboriginal and Torres Strait Islander Services (ATSIS). Since 2004, many Indigenous community organisations have continued to receive funding to provide services. NGOs from outside remote communities have increasingly been funded by government to provide services to remote communities. The main types of organisations funded by governments to deliver services in remote areas are community councils/corporations, regional service providers, and specialised service providers. Many of the organisations are relatively small and very few specialise in a single area of service delivery (Office of Evaluation and Audit (Indigenous Programs) 2009). The most developed community services tend to be in the area of primary health care (Mason 2006).

Historically, Community Development Employment Projects (CDEP) organisations have delivered a range of services in remotes communities. As of the 1 July 2013, the CDEP scheme was replaced by the Remote Jobs and Communities Program, combining four programs currently providing employment and participation services and community development in remote Australia (see Department of Social Services 2013). These are existing CDEP providers, Job Services Australia, Disability Employment Services, and the Indigenous Employment Program.

There are a number of features of Indigenous communities in remote and very remote areas of Australia which make delivering services difficult and expensive. These include small populations, low population density, long distances, extreme seasonal variation in weather, insufficient accessible and affordable transport, physical isolation, and poor-quality infrastructure. Other challenges are related to the characteristics of the Indigenous population and the negative experiences that many Indigenous people have had in their interactions with government agencies. These have been discussed in Chapter 1.

In response to the concerns regarding the lack of access to services and poor coordination of services in remote communities, a number of government initiatives are being implemented which aim to improve service delivery in these communities. One initiative being implemented is the National Partnership Agreement on Remote Service Delivery (NPARSD), a place-based approach, which involves the designation of 29 priority communities or locations. It is designed to both improve the range and standard of services delivered, and to improve community engagement and development. The 29 priority communities are spread across New South Wales, Queensland, South Australia, Western Australia and the Northern Territory, and will be the focus of targeted improvements in government service delivery.

These are among the larger communities in remote areas of Australia and provide a good guide as to the number of people who may be eligible for the NDIS in this community type. Population projections for 2026 have been undertaken for these communities by the Centre for Aboriginal Economic Policy Research (CAEPR), and this analysis is presented below.[5]

Cost of providing services according to Indigenous status and geographic remoteness

The costs of providing many services increase with geographic remoteness. The Commonwealth Grants Commission (CGC) provides estimates of how the costs per employee vary according to geographic remoteness for police, schools and general services. The CGC estimate of the remoteness cost gradient of providing government services is shown in Fig. 5.1. It is clear that the relative cost per employee increases sharply with remoteness. The cost-remoteness gradient is steepest for police, followed by schools and then general services. In remote areas the cost per employee of providing policing is over 1.5 times that in a highly accessible area, whereas the costs of providing general services in very remote areas is just under 1.2 times the cost in highly accessible areas.

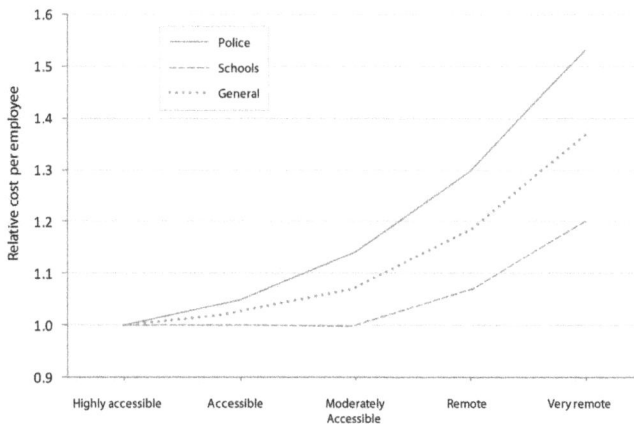

Fig. 5.1 Remoteness cost gradient for government services, Australia, 2012

Source: CGC 2012: Fig. 5.4

5   In late 2009, CAEPR was commissioned by FaHCSIA to undertake population projections for the 29 NPARSD communities. Details of the method used to produce the population projections are provided in Appendix 1 (projection scenario 4 has been used).

Even after the additional costs associated with geographic isolation are taken into account, the CGC finds that on average more is spent on Indigenous people than on comparable non-Indigenous people. CGC estimates indicate that on average, States/Territories spend four times as much on welfare and housing services for Indigenous people as they spend on non-Indigenous people with the same remoteness and other socio-demographic attributes (Table 5.1).

Table 5.1 Estimated average spending on comparable Indigenous and non-Indigenous people, Australia, 2012[a]

Service	Average spending per Indigenous person ($)	Average spending on comparable non-Indigenous people ($)	Ratio
Schools education	5 375	3 206	1.7
Post school education	667	237	2.8
Admitted patients	2 836	1 089	2.6
Community health	1 914	842	2.3
Welfare and housing	5 995	1 379	4.3
Services to communities	1 448	789	1.8
Justice services	4 988	713	7.0
Other	4 101	4 101	1.0
Total	27 325	12 356	2.2

a. The average spending on non-Indigenous people weighted by the socio-demographic mix of the Indigenous population.

Source: CGC 2012: Table 5.5

Estimating current and projected demand for NDIS in NPARSD locations

As discussed above, the 29 priority communities identified under NPARSD provide a useful basis for examining how the NDIS may impact in some remote communities. Using existing data sets, it is not possible to estimate reliably the rate of disability for the NPARSD communities (see Chapter 2). Therefore, in order to produce indicative estimates of the level of disability in the NPARSD communities, the following rough calculation is used. Based upon the Productivity Commission Report, the estimated Tier 3 NDIS population is 410 000, which is 2.12 per cent of the Australian population aged 65 years and under in 2010. This NDIS coverage rate is then multiplied by 2.5, our best estimation of the relative difference in the rate of disability between Indigenous and non-Indigenous Australians (see Chapter 2). The estimated Indigenous NDIS coverage rate is therefore 5.3 per cent, which is applied to the estimated Indigenous population aged 0–64 years in the 29 communities, as well as the projected 2026 population.

The estimates and projections presented in Table 5.2 show that for a number of the larger NPARSD communities there is a substantial number of Indigenous Australians who potentially fall under the remit of the NDIS. It is estimated that by 2026 there will be 2 755 people living in the NPARSD communities who would have significant and permanent disability and be eligible for the NDIS, ranging from 16 in Mossman Gorge to 255 in Maningrida.

The Productivity Commission cost estimates of their proposed scheme are based on an average individual package value of about $29 000 per annum.[6] Multiplying this by the relative cost ratio of 1.2 used by the CGC (2012) for remote Australia results in an estimated expenditure of about $35 000 per potential NDIS user in a remote community and rises to about $40 000 in very remote areas. To the extent that in these communities there is relatively little payment made for disability services, the introduction of the NDIS will potentially lead to a considerable inflow of funds into many of the large communities. For example, based on these projections it is estimated that by 2026 an additional $8.8 million per annum (in 2012 dollars) in NDIS funding will be coming into Maningrida.

The CGC also includes an additional estimate for higher average spending across a range of services for Indigenous compared to non-Indigenous users. This is in addition to differences based on socioeconomic status and remoteness of the area in which that service is provided. For community health, the ratio was 2.3 times higher for an Indigenous compared to a non-Indigenous person. For welfare and housing, it was 4.3 times as high. If these were also applied to services as part of the NDIS then it is quite possible that additional expenditure in some of the larger communities could be in the tens of millions of dollars.

---

6   This was derived by dividing the total estimated expenditure on the care and support component of the scheme ($1.184 billion) by the Tier 3 NDIS population (410 000).

Table 5.2 Potential NDIS demand in 29 priority communities, Australia, 2006–2026

Community	State	2006 estimate			2026 projection		
		Total	Aged 0–64 years	Potential NDIS demand	Total	Aged 0–64 years	Potential NDIS demand
Amata	SA	341	328	17	657	607	32
Angurugu	NT	1 013	990	52	1 958	1 823	97
Ardyaloon	WA	243	235	12	467	430	23
Aurukun	Qld	1 059	1 026	54	2 051	1 875	99
Beagle Bay	WA	1 059	1 026	54	2 051	1 875	99
Coen	Qld	239	232	12	466	427	23
Doomadgee	Qld	1 102	1 067	57	2 168	2 007	106
Fitzroy Crossing	WA	733	697	37	1 454	1 354	72
Galiwinku	NT	2 158	2 110	112	4 178	3 891	206
Gapuwiyak	NT	1 208	1 180	63	2 336	2 175	115
Gunbalanya	NT	1 141	1 116	59	2 243	2 111	112
Halls Creek	WA	1 092	1 047	56	2 145	1 994	106
Hermannsburg	NT	938	904	48	1 798	1 673	89
Hope Vale	Qld	797	772	41	1 543	1 411	75
Lajamanu	NT	735	711	38	1 427	1 337	71
Maningrida	NT	2 600	2 545	135	5 111	4 811	255
Milingimbi	NT	1 086	1 063	56	2 132	2 007	106
Mimili	SA	289	278	15	558	515	27
Mornington Island	Qld	1 028	995	53	2 026	1 875	99
Mossman Gorge	Qld	165	160	8	327	302	16
Nguiu	NT	1 463	1 432	76	2 875	2 706	143
Ngukurr	NT	1 055	1 021	54	2 043	1 914	101
Numbulwar	NT	713	697	37	1 381	1 286	68
Umbakumba	NT	434	424	22	839	782	41
Wadeye	NT	2 074	2 030	108	4 077	3 838	203
Walgett	NSW	1 220	1 174	62	2 429	2 220	118
Wilcannia	NSW	453	436	23	888	811	43
Yirrkala	NT	1 472	1 438	76	2 857	2 662	141
Yuendumu	NT	701	675	36	1 348	1 255	67
Total		28 612	27 808	1 474	55 832	51 971	2 755

Source: Customised calculations based on 2006 Census data, details given in Appendix 1

Primary health care system in remote communities

One of the best developed and the most extensive service system in remote communities is the primary health care system. The experience has been that standard mainstream services do not meet the needs of rural and remote communities (Humphreys and Wakerman 2008). This has led to a range of different and distinctive models for the delivery of services. Humphreys and Wakerman (2008) have developed a useful typology (reproduced in Table 5.3) for models for the delivery of primary health care in rural and remote communities.

Table 5.3 Typology of 'innovative' rural and remote models for primary health care delivery

Context: rural-remote continuum	Primary health care model & examples	Main drivers for model
RURAL Larger, more closely settled communities	Discrete services: • 'Walk-in/walk-out' model • Viable models of General Practice • University Clinics	Population numbers usually sufficient to meet essential service requirements (some supports still needed to address workforce recruitment and retention)
	Integrated Services • shared care • Coordinated Care Trials • Public Health Service teams • multi-purpose services	Service integration resulting from pooled funding maximises efficiencies and access to locally available services. Single point of entry to the health system helps to coordinate patient care and reduces the need for travel
	Comprehensive Public Health Service services: • Aboriginal Controlled Community Health Services	Community participation, service flexibility to meet local circumstances, and access to services are critical components where few alternative ways of delivering appropriate care exist
REMOTE Small populations dispersed over vast areas	Outreach Services: • 'hub and spoke' models • visiting services • 'fly-in, fly-out' services • telehealth/telemedicine	Periodic outreach services (sometimes co-existing with other models) provide care to communities too small to support permanent local services

Source: Humphreys and Wakerman 2008: 6

While a number of innovative models have been developed and implemented, Humphreys and Wakerman (2008: 7) conclude that 'few have been evaluated in terms of their impact on health outcomes'. Barriers to the provision of health services to regional and remote communities which have been identified include:

- a funding focus on remunerating service providers rather than the needs of consumers which can result in supplier-induced demand

- workforce shortages

- inadequate health service performance monitoring and evaluation

- failure to organise care for chronic conditions

- failure to address prevention adequately

- lack of infrastructure, and

- failure to empower patients to participate in their care.

Many of these issues are directly applicable to the provision of disability services. A feature of health services in remote communities is that organisations typically provide a wider range of services than health services in urban areas. In rural and remote areas they often provide community-wide integrated health services that can include mental health, oral health, community, and aged care and social services (see *The National Strategic Framework for Rural and Remote Health* between the Commonwealth, and State and the Northern Territory Governments by the Rural Health Standing Committee (Rural and Regional Health Australia 2012)).

Models for the delivery of family and relationship services in regional, rural and remote areas

An alternative typology of service provider models developed in the context of the delivery of family and relationship services in regional, rural and remote areas has been developed by Roufeil and Battye (2008). Table 5.4 provides an overview of common service provider models operating in regional, rural and remote Australia and their advantages and disadvantages. The authors note that there is limited published research comparing the effectiveness of different models, and have called for evaluations to be better funded and integrated into programs. In most cases, however, there is some evidence on how to maximise the efficacy of particular service models. Roufeil and Battye (2008) also state that while it is useful to consider different types of service models, it is important to keep in mind that the most critical requirement in rural, regional and remote communities is having strong, broad-based generalist services and that there are clear disadvantages in locating specialist services in such areas if there is not also a strong generalist workforce.

Table 5.4 Review of service provider models in regional, rural and remote areas of Australia

Model	Characteristics	Advantages	Disadvantages
Purchaser-provider	The purchaser is generally the government, which specifies the type, level, target groups and location of a service that is subsequently delivered by an auspice body (the provider); usually involves a fixed-term contract.	Provides an effective way to distribute finite funds. Potentially facilitates delivery of services by local people, as opposed to introducing new services to a town. It is preferable if purchaser and provider are able to be flexible with the specified service guidelines so that local needs can be accommodated.	Tender process fosters competition, not cooperation, between agencies. Tenders are skewed towards being granted on grounds of pricing, not on basis of local knowledge. Contract usually developed off-site and rarely reflects local needs (can be overcome by requiring tenderers to tailor service to meet local needs). Many providers are urban-based, with exogenous service delivery leading to loss of local trust, reduced local knowledge, diminished local capacity-building and reduced options for local cowmmunity development. Rigid adherence by purchaser to specified services and target groups limits ability of provider to implement flexible and holistic services to families.
Hub and spoke	A way of facilitating regionalisation and centralisation of services, such that services tend to be based in areas of greatest population density (hub) and provide services out to smaller centres (spokes). Can operate under a variety of funding models, including purchaser-provider.	Makes economic sense; works well when outreach services are regular, reliable, and adequately resourced, and have sufficient time to engage with local community.	Many outreach services are unreliable and susceptible to the vagaries of the weather, transport and availability of staff. Outsider providers often have little local knowledge and lack community trust. Managers are generally isolated from spokes, with little local knowledge.

Model	Characteristics	Advantages	Disadvantages
Collaborative models: interagency collaboration/ networking	Interagency collaboration spans informal networks (e.g. knowing who to talk to in order to reduce red tape) and formal networks (e.g. partnerships in service delivery using existing networks, referral protocols, case conferences, memoranda of understanding, co-location, and joint training).	Scarce resources can be maximised to produce the critical mass needed to sustain effective service delivery (e.g. *Bila Muuji Social and Emotional Wellbeing Initiative*). Fosters holistic approach to assisting families. Collaboration builds trust and a culture of reciprocity between providers and communities. Collaboration becomes increasingly important as remoteness increases. Although partnerships involve non-local educators, local agencies conducting the promotion/practical setup can help to ameliorate concerns about confidentiality (e.g. Lutheran Community Care's *Through Thick and Thin* program). Works best with active managerial support, time allocation, and strong leadership/role modelling.	Collaboration and effective networking challenges frontline staff, management and organisations; work overload often distracts from collaborative approach. Attitudes toward interagency collaboration at local level can be negatively influenced by competitive tendering processes.
Collaborative models: co-location	Sharing expensive infrastructure between agencies.	Useful for small agencies that would otherwise spend a high proportion of budget on infrastructure. Can be a valuable one-stop shop for clients (e.g. Early Years Centre in Nerang, Queensland).	Research evidence of efficacy of co-location is equivocal and co-location alone is probably insufficient to improve service delivery. Co-located agencies in small communities are vulnerable if one of the participating agencies closes. One-stop shops rarely overcome tyranny of distance for rural or remote communities.

Model	Characteristics	Advantages	Disadvantages
Collaborative models: fund blending	A type of collaborative model that involves one agency receiving funds from multiple sources to create a resource pool, with staff straddling various programs.	Potential to create a critical mass of resources that might otherwise be impossible to develop. Fosters mutual support between staff and decreases professional isolation. Most successful if multi-party agreements, including mechanisms for reporting, are established prior to model implementation.	Demanding and time-consuming for management and staff to report to several funding bodies. Being answerable to multiple funding bodies with inflexible program requirements can impact on agency sustainability in the long term.
Technology-based models	Spans a range of programs delivered by various technologies, including telephone, email counselling, chat rooms and videoconferencing. Often a mix of self-help and e-technology support.	Ease of access for clients in some regional, rural and remote communities. May facilitate service use in rural regions, due to increased anonymity of client. Appears to be useful for facilitating staff professional development, but evidence base still developing for delivery of many therapeutic programs. Some evidence supporting telephone delivery of non-structured services, and more structured services.	Access to cheap, reliable and efficient Internet service is highly variable across Australia. Need to develop evidence of efficacy of programs developed for face-to-face delivery when implemented via various technologies. Delivery of services using various technologies often requires staff to acquire new skills. It can take considerable time to train and support workers and develop appropriate usage policies that address the issue of confidentiality.
Pilot and seed funding	One-off funding for a specified service. This is not really a service model, but a funding stream. It is included here due to the high prevalence of services operating in an rural, remote and regional capacity.	Helps to establish a much needed service. Works best when there is a mechanism for ongoing funding to be readily available if the program is successful and the pilot funding accurately reflects the cost of running the service.	Communities highly suspicious of these funding arrangements, given the preponderance of rural, remote and regional services that are set up and then dismantled due to lack of funds, a situation that has eroded community trust in local agencies.

Source: Roufeil and Battye 2008: Table 1

6. Existing evaluations of service delivery models

There is very little Australian research on the pros and cons of different models of disability service provision in terms of their impact on Indigenous people. There is, however, some research which provides insights into Indigenous experiences of disability and related service usage, as well as the extent to which this differs to that of other Australians. Much of this has already been touched on in this monograph. This chapter expands upon these issues.

A relatively comprehensive review of Australian research was undertaken for this monograph. While selected international research was reviewed, a more comprehensive assessment of international research was beyond the scope of this exercise. Program and service descriptions were found to be more common than impact evaluations. This reflects to a certain extent the difficulty of evaluating programs that provide services in such a challenging environment. Furthermore, where impact evaluations were attempted, data gaps and discrepancies often limited the evaluation's validity. Therefore, although examples of promising practice and areas of ongoing challenge did emerge from the literature review, findings must be interpreted with a level of caution.

Successful replication or scaling-up of service delivery models often requires detailed knowledge of the context in which models apply, the populations to which they apply, and the specific mechanisms within programs that have achieved the reported results (Pawson and Tilley 2004). Some of the cases of promising practice identified in the review of the literature for this monograph have emerged from overseas models where the contexts are only partially comparable, and the mechanisms may not be fully explicated. Also, some models had been tested only in remote contexts and others only in urban contexts. Service providers were often the focus of research, likely due at least in part to the difficulties of accessing people with disabilities and their carers. Remote and Indigenous populations posed a particular challenge for researchers. In a few cases, research instruments were specifically designed to respond to cultural and remote Indigenous community needs, or to the special needs of Indigenous people with disability and their carers. However, it was difficult to find good examples of evaluations that employed program logic or quantitative impact measures, and even these often struggled with accessing reliable data and reconciling it with qualitative data.

While there have been evaluations of consumer-directed disability models and evaluations of Indigenous-targeted disability services, there is little in the literature that discusses the impact of consumer-directed disability models for Indigenous peoples. The minor exception to this is the Services Our Way program of New South Wales, which shows promise in this regard. Some of the reasons for this gap in the literature will emerge from the discussion below.

There have been several studies of the experience of Indigenous people with disability services. A review of access by Indigenous people to the New South Wales government program Ageing, Disability and Home Care (ADHC) by the New South Wales Ombudsman (2010: 5) found that:

> Despite the relatively high rate of disability in Aboriginal communities, the most common theme that emerged during our review was the lack of knowledge and understanding within Aboriginal communities about ADHC and the disability service system—in particular, the services available to Aboriginal people with a disability and their families, and the availability of specific entitlements.

The review by the NSW Ombudsman (2010) also reported that many service providers and community members had told them that the types of support wanted by many Indigenous people with a disability differed to those sought by non-Indigenous people. Specifically, Indigenous people with a disability tended to be more likely to want what one might call practical help. Examples listed included assistance to replace whitegoods, pay for car registration or petrol, or to allow the family to take a holiday together for respite. It was reported that Indigenous people tend to want to take a break with their family members and to be supported by a carer rather than the family member with a disability being placed in centre-based respite care.

While the review of the existing research identified several studies of Indigenous experiences with disability services, this is a question on which there has been relatively little research. Better understanding of Indigenous experiences with disability services and the nature of services which best meet the specific needs of Indigenous people with a disability is an area in which further research is needed in order to inform the design of the NDIS. A study of formal individual advocacy services (paid advocates employed by an advocacy agency, working with people with disability on short-term and issue-specific bases) found that in Indigenous communities advocates assist people with a disability by linking the person with other services and, in particular, helping those who are unable to or would never read information, or who are not aware of the services that are available (Jenny Pearson & Associates Pty Ltd 2009).

A consistent theme in reviews of the experience of Indigenous people with disability services is that there is a lack of knowledge and understanding within the Indigenous community about the disability service system and the services available to Indigenous people with a disability and their families (NSW Ombudsman 2010).

In 2008, the Australian Government released a discussion paper asking community members to respond to a series of questions about their experience of disability. The purpose of the consultations was to inform the development of a national disability strategy. More than 750 submissions were received. An analysis of the submissions has been undertaken (National People with Disabilities and Carer Council 2009). Key themes were identified from the submissions that are directly related to Indigenous people.

- Few disability service providers seem to grasp the complexity of the issues confronting Indigenous people.

- Mainstream services targeting Indigenous people do not always understand the specific issues facing Indigenous Australians with disabilities and their families.

- The chronic lack of services in regional and remote areas not only restricts choice but sometimes means people are forced to leave their communities in order to access services and support. For some people this means onerous and expensive travel over several days of the week. For others, particularly in Indigenous communities, it has meant the dislocation of families to enable the person to receive treatment.

- The importance of greater availability of transport to improve access to health care and other services and support was a recurring theme.

- The specific needs of Indigenous carers are often neglected, and there is a pressing need for greater availability of respite.

- It is often difficult for people with disabilities to participate fully in important cultural activities. Aboriginal and Torres Strait Islander people with disabilities who want to be full and active participants in the life of their community often find themselves isolated and excluded.

The NSW Ombudsman's review of 2010 identified a range of attitudinal factors that impact on Indigenous people's ability and willingness to seek assistance. These include:

- being unable to relate to the concept of disability

- variable understandings in and among Aboriginal communities about what constitutes a disability

- a belief that there is a cultural obligation to care for a person with a disability within the family

- wanting to avoid the label of 'disability' due to a perception that there is a stigma attached to it

- mistrust of government agencies.[1]

The fear of losing children with special needs to service providers may be particularly acute. One reason given for the under-use of services is negative past experiences with government services, notably where these involve outsiders entering an individual's home. As observed earlier, concerns were raised that care workers who entered an Indigenous person's home, for respite care for example, would be disparaging of the person regarding the cleanliness of their home (King 2010: 205).

The presence of Indigenous staff is said to encourage service access (Western Australia Disability Services Commission 2006). However, one study found that while Indigenous people in urban areas frequently preferred to use services with Indigenous staff members, there were others who preferred other services. Several reasons were given for this. In some cases it was because the person felt that these other services offered better care provision. In other cases people raised the issue of confidentiality, suggesting that they tended to stay away from services that had Indigenous staff members because of the potential that they may have some form of relationship with these individuals.

The importance of consultation with Indigenous people as services are being designed rather than simply imposing a model upon the community is often emphasised. However, consultation fatigue can result, particularly where input does not lead to action. One interesting model for people with a disability gave participants an opportunity to access individual advocacy support so that they saw the engagement as meeting their needs as well as an opportunity to offer information (Aboriginal Disability Network New South Wales 2012). Although consultation may in some cases mean providing input to decision-makers who will then design service models, in a number of cases more collaborative service design models have emerged. True partnership is not easy to achieve; Burton (2012) profiles nine partnerships between Indigenous and mainstream agencies, highlighting elements of promising practice but also noting the challenges involved.

---

1   This issue is discussed in a number of government service planning documents, e.g. Victorian Auditor-General's Office 2011; Western Australia Disability Services Commission 2006.

An additional factor identified in the review was the complex interaction between imprisonment and disability. The rate of imprisonment of Indigenous people is much higher than for the Australian population as a whole. The ABS (2012c: 49) reports that:

> The age standardised imprisonment rate for Aboriginal and Torres Strait Islander prisoners at 30 June 2012 was 1 914 Aboriginal and Torres Strait Islander prisoners per 100 000 adult Aboriginal and Torres Strait Islander population. The equivalent rate for non-Indigenous prisoners was 129 non-Indigenous prisoners per 100 000 adult non-Indigenous population.

The same data indicates that some 5–7 per cent of the Indigenous male population aged 20–44 years are imprisoned at any one time. While the evidence on Indigenous prisoners with a disability is limited, research conducted in Victorian prisons has found that Indigenous prisoners are more likely to have an intellectual disability than are non-Indigenous prisoners (Holland et al. 2007). Some types of impairment found particularly commonly in Australian Indigenous populations are over-represented in prison populations, such as cognitive impairments, Acquired Brain Injury, and hearing impairments. These conditions may be disproportionately linked to criminal activity and recidivism, and hence special support may be required to end this cycle. The point though is that it will be important to consider how the NDIS operates for people with a disability who are entering and leaving prison.

Examples of disability services models

This section provides some examples of disability services models. Each is a different model, but all offer findings relevant to service provision to Indigenous Australians with disabilities. The first is a program operating in Canadian Aboriginal communities, most of them remote. The program has been extensively evaluated, and has been found effective in building services and a workforce in areas where none previously existed. The second is an Australian program of individual funding packages targeted at Aboriginal people with disabilities in New South Wales, including metropolitan areas.

First Nations and Inuit Home and Community Care Program

The First Nations and Inuit Home and Community Care (FNIHCC) Program is a Canadian program targeted at that country's Aboriginal population. In terms of the models set out above, it offers block funding through contribution agreements and is administered by Aboriginal governance bodies, using funds pooled from two different government agencies that enable staff to work across service boundaries. It is targeted in large part at building service provision capacity in regions where there have historically been few or no services.

FNIHCC is available only to Inuit living in an Inuit settlement, to First Nations people living on reserves south of 60° North latitude, or in First Nations communities north of 60°. Designed to work in partnership with Aboriginal communities to maximise the ability of people requiring care to remain in their own homes, FNIHCC was first established in 1999. It has since been extensively evaluated, with evaluations released in 2001, 2005, and 2008; examples of particularly promising practice within specific FNIHCC programs were published in 2010 (Canadian Home Care Association 2010; Health Canada 2008). FNIHCC clients can be of any age, but must have been formally assessed to require one or more essential services, and it must be determined that the services can be provided with reasonable safety to both the client and caregiver. Funds are held by the local Aboriginal governance body, such as a Band Council, and are allocated based on assessment of need.

Early reports and evaluations of the program focused on establishment processes such as need assessment, funding formulas, community education and workforce training. Issues identified in this stage included the difficulties experienced by smaller more remote communities. Smaller communities (i.e., those under 1 000 people) had greater difficulty in finding the human resources to conduct needs assessments and felt disadvantaged by fixed funding formulae. Remote communities experienced difficulty in securing personnel, and found that resourcing did not take into account the additional transport costs they faced. Furthermore, one of the key issues identified was the challenge involved in implementing a nationally consistent model over a diverse set of communities. Again, smaller and more remote communities faced greater challenges.

The most recent evaluation (Health Canada 2008) found once again that FNIHCC had achieved much, continued to be needed, and recommended that its funding continue. It has built a workforce and provided services in regions where none had previously existed. According to some types of data, hospital admissions were down and costs decreased due to improved local care (e.g. lower numbers of amputations). Aboriginal community members appreciated being able to stay in their home community for services delivered in their own language. However, half of those interviewed responded that the program was not entirely culturally appropriate, particularly where off-reserve providers were involved. Some wanted traditional healers included in the program.

Aboriginal communities in the southern regions, closer to major metropolitan areas, experienced better outcomes than more northerly, remote communities.

Band Councils sometimes had fixed ideas about which types of disability services were most important. In one case (Durst, Gay and Morin 2006), a woman left for an urban area when she was unable to get funding allocated for a ramp to her house. In some communities, where aged care was assumed by the Band Council to be the priority need, there was concern that children's disabilities were being under-served.

One important finding was that the model had changed over time. Acute care, particularly transitional care after hospital discharge, was becoming more frequent. The same personnel and procedures were typically required for transitional care and for long term disabilities, so this model appeared to be cost-effective. It indicates, in fact, that adhering to a strictly disability focused model may not be as cost-effective in remote communities as a more flexible model, perhaps redefining disability to encompass short-term as well as longer-term conditions. However, while this improved service and cost effectiveness, it complicated the accountability requirements, as it was not easy to distinguish between services delivered from each pool of funding, and both government agencies required reporting for their own funds.

Finally, it was not easy for the evaluators to reconcile data from the qualitative and from the quantitative sections of the evaluation, demonstrating the importance of setting up data systems from the outset that allow for improvement as well as accountability.

Services Our Way

Many Australian jurisdictions have instituted individual funding models for people with disabilities, but few appear to have been targeted specifically at Indigenous Australians. One relatively recent exception is the Services Our Way (SOW) program of New South Wales. While the program is too recent to have been formally evaluated in as much detail as the FNIHCC, there are a number of features of SOW that are worth noting.

The program commenced in the Shoalhaven in 2010–11 as a demonstration project. The program is available to Aboriginal people with a diagnosed intellectual or physical disability, including Acquired Brain Injury and Multiple Sclerosis. SOW principles state that the program is family-centred, strengths-based and culturally appropriate, working collaboratively with other human service organisations and with Aboriginal communities. It encompasses prevention and early intervention, with a deliberately broad interpretation of disability.

In terms of the models set out above, it is an individual support funding package with the funds held by the agency. A key component of SOW is that it is an

Aboriginal program delivered by Aboriginal Support Specialists for Aboriginal people with a disability, their carers and families. Aboriginal people with a disability and their families are able to choose how much help they get from Aboriginal Support Specialists in terms of the level of support and assistance. This Aboriginal Support Specialist is available to provide as much or as little support in developing a 6–12 months Support Plan as desired. However, the Aboriginal Support Specialist always manages funding, with all invoices and receipts sent to them.

Not only is disability interpreted broadly, but so are the types of supports that can be purchased. While there is still a focus on traditional supports (such as respite, personal care, day programs, and therapy) clients are encouraged to think in creative ways in term of service provision. Carers within the scheme can have a range of relationships with the person with a disability, including as a parent, grandparent, family member, extended family member or other person with cultural obligations to provide care for the person. There are a number of constraints on spending, including prohibitions on using the funds for gambling or for support of family members other than the person with a disability and their primary carer. These constraints aside, there are a range of possible supports listed in the guidelines which include:

- support for access to community and recreation opportunities, e.g. transport and tickets/entry fees

- supplementation of the transport costs of the person with a disability, where these costs are not fully covered by other schemes

- goods or supports from other community or government programs if the person is otherwise unable to access these goods or supports in a timely manner

- selected household items that are otherwise not affordable and will relieve stress and/or enhance capacity

- supports or resources to increase networking, caring skills, communication, access to ideas and/or improving lifestyle routines

- a service that can build access and inclusion to specific places/activities by addressing physical, attitudinal, and skill barriers.

While there have been few formal evaluations of the program, storytelling and action-based research are being used to assess and improve the program. According to comments from relevant New South Wales government officials, implementation of the demonstration project in the Southern Region thus far has presented a number of consistent findings. These findings provide insight into Aboriginal people with a disability and their families' interaction with the disability service system.

- Many of the clients, approximately 90 per cent, are young children, and have been diagnosed with either autism or an intellectual disability.

- Some clients have not accessed disability services previously and therefore do not have a legitimate medical diagnosis to ensure eligibility, which can delay access to services.

- Many of the clients are reluctant to access structured overnight, centre-based respite services, continue to have difficulty accessing such services, and are confronted with an inflexible and culturally inappropriate service response.

- Significant funding otherwise used for individualised support packages is being unnecessarily diverted to access centre-based respite services.

- A Parents of Children with Autism Support Group has been established and the families have benefited positively from group forums to discuss their experiences and thoughts about disability and caring, and have suggested innovative solutions to respite services.

- Many of the clients and their families were unfamiliar with these services and the technologies available to support their adolescent children, e.g. automated wheelchairs, voice recognition technology, and the use of computers in developing support plans.

- Parents have commented on the difference it makes working with an Aboriginal Support Specialist who understands the cultural complexities of Aboriginal families.

- The clients and their families are innovative with the individualised disability plans.

Given the similarities between the SOW program and the way in which the NDIS is likely to be applied, it will be important to learn from identified strengths and weaknesses of the program.

7. Providing a disability workforce

Irrespective of the service delivery model used, the increased demand for disability services resulting from the increased funding will require a substantial increase in the disability care workforce. The move towards a greater level of consumer control is likely to also result in changes in the particular services provided and hence in the skill composition of the disability workforce. While the NDIS will mostly expand employment of existing job types, one new role that will be created as part of the NDIS is that of local area coordinator. This person will act as the main contact point between the system and people with disabilities (Productivity Commission 2011: 744). As the NDIS expands it is likely that local area coordinators will be able to specialise in specific types of disability, differing levels of functional impairment, specific types of support needs, different cultural groups and different backgrounds. However there is likely to be less possibility for specialisation in more remote areas of Australia (Productivity Commission 2011: 745). The NDIS would also need to employ assessors, most likely experienced allied health professionals, to determine people's needs and tailor care packages for them (Productivity Commission 2011: 746).

Economic theory suggests that the increased demand for services will initially lead to an increase in the price of disability services. The increase in price stimulates an increase in the supply of disability services as existing providers expand their supply of services or new providers enter the market. The extent to which this increase in demand leads to an increase in the supply of disability services will depend in large part on how fast the supply of workers in the industry is able to increase; staffing costs are a high proportion of the costs for most types of disability services. With the pressure of an increasing and ageing population as well as demand for the same workers in other industries, there is the strong potential for significant labour shortages. If there are labour shortages, the level of services across Australia would be unlikely to increase substantially, with increases in demand leading to an increase in prices as well as a reallocation of services into more affluent areas.

In a review of the literature, Mason (2006) identified the lack of a strong theoretical base around the provision of social care services in rural and remote Australia. There were, however, a number of key issues that she touched upon. The first of these was a widespread feeling that urbo-centrism—the assumption that the city or urban environment is the norm—precluded an appropriate delivery of services. From a workforce point of view, this meant that there was a lack of recognition that 'specialisation is alien to rural culture, where rural people are expected to improvise and come up with practical solutions themselves' (Mason 2006: 44).

Another factor that is noted as being substantially different in a rural or remote context compared to urban areas is the blurring of the boundaries between work and non-work hours. Rural social care workers are more likely to be on call than those in urban parts of the country, although this is not always officially recognised. Writing with regard to rural health workers, Birks et al. (2010) note that 'nurses in small or isolated communities are effectively on call 24 hours a day, seven days a week, irrespective of rosters...and that this constitutes a major source of stress'. Furthermore, the culture in many rural areas is said to be such that members of the workforce find it difficult to do their job adequately without a significant degree of social interaction. According to Mason (2006: 45) 'the traditional professional tenets about keeping the relationship with the client on a strongly formal basis cannot easily be applied in a rural practice'. These additional pressures on the disability workforce of working in regional, rural and remote areas need to be taken into account when designing the NDIS.

The current disability workforce

While the precise number of workers in the disability care sector is unknown, it is estimated that around 68 700 workers (34 000 full-time equivalent (FTE) positions) provide disability services or manage those who do so (Productivity Commission 2011: 695). It is estimated that there are 20 people with a disability for each FTE worker in the sector. However, because not all of those with a disability access services, there are in effect only about five users of disability services per worker.

Workers in the disability support care sector can be categorised into three broad categories:

- non-professionals, including carers, home care workers, community care workers and disability or residential support workers (62% of the workforce)

- professionals, including allied health workers, social workers and disability case managers (12% of the workforce)

- managers and administrators (25% of the workforce).

Around three-quarters of those within the disability support care sector are employed by not-for-profit service providers, with the government and private for-profit sector agencies employing the remainder (Productivity Commission

2011). Over 80 per cent of disability workers are women. Additionally, relative to the overall Australian workforce; a much higher proportion of workers in the disability sector are aged 40–59 years, and a smaller proportion are less than 30 years of age. than is the case for the Australian labour force in general (Productivity Commission 2011).

On average, workers in the sector receive relatively low wages. There is, however, significant variation within the sector, with those workers employed by the government earning more than those in the non-government sector (Productivity Commission 2011). In many surveys of the disability labour force, wanting to help others is often cited as the main motivation for work in the sector, while pay is never ranked highly. Satisfaction with pay is lower than for other industries (Productivity Commission 2011). It should be noted, though, that this situation may change with the recent Social and Community Services award decision by Fair Work Australia in February 2012.

Relative to the rest of the workforce, a much higher proportion of disability workers are engaged in part-time or casual jobs and many (around one-quarter) work more than one job (Productivity Commission 2011: 700). The ability to work part-time is also a potential motivation for people working in the industry, with community services workers working 31 hours per week on average, compared with 37 hours for all people employed in all occupations. Females worked fewer hours per week than males, with over half of employed females (56.2%) working less than 35 hours per week, compared to 39.9 per cent of males in community services (AIHW 2009b).

Almost two-thirds (64.1%) of community services workers reported having completed a non-school qualification. The most common highest qualification among community services workers was a certificate (36.1% of those who reported having a qualification). The distribution of qualification level differed across the occupations. Family services, disability and other community services managers were more likely to hold a bachelor degree (47.3%, 35.4% and 39.4% respectively) than another qualification. By contrast, aged and/or disabled care workers (67.7%) typically held a certificate (AIHW 2009b: 25).

Current labour shortages

In recent years there has been an increase in government spending on disability services. This has resulted in the number of aged and/or disability care workers increasing from around 37 000 in 1996 to about 81 000 in 2006 (AIHW 2009b). The increase in the size of the workforce was not spread evenly across the country and there are conflicting reports of labour shortages already occurring in the sector. Some organisations, including those contacted for this monograph, report significant difficulties in finding suitably qualified workers. However, in a recent survey 26 per cent of workers said they wanted to increase their hours, contradicting to a certain extent reports of a shortage (Productivity Commission 2011: 704).

It may be that there are geographic rigidities with many workers unable to move to areas where labour shortages are most acute. This is quite possible given the relatively low wages and part-time hours in the industry, meaning that those in the industry are less likely to be the primary earner in the household (and hence are tied to the area in which their spouse or partner reside).

In 2006, there were 1 422 workers in community services occupations per 100 000 residents. The highest number per 100 000 population was in the Northern Territory (1 817), followed by the Australian Capital Territory (1 749). The lowest number was in New South Wales where there were 1 290 community services workers per 100 000 of population. Across occupations, child and youth services workers had the highest national number, followed by aged and/or disabled care workers (570 and 392 workers per 100 000 of population respectively). The pattern was reversed in Tasmania and South Australia, where the child and youth services worker rates (517 and 576 respectively) were lower than their respective aged and/or disabled care worker rates (699 and 593) (AIHW 2009b: 41). Overall, there were 184 disability services workers per 100 000 of population (AIHW 2009b: 39).

Community services workers were more evenly spread across the Remoteness Areas than health workers. The highest number of workers per 100 000 was in 'very remote Australia' (1 696), followed by 'inner regional' Australia (1 541) (AIHW 2009b: Table 4.2). The figures for the other areas were: 'outer regional' 1 443; 'remote' 1 407; and 'major cities' the lowest, 1 379 workers per 100 000 of population. While there were a greater number of community service workers (per 100 000 persons) in 'very remote' areas, this does not mean that the availability of community service workers for the typical resident in these areas was as high as in other locations. This is because those who make use of these community service workers would need to travel much greater distances to access them. This is made clear in Table 7.1, below, which uses a slightly different classification of disability and related workers, generated for this monograph, and looks specifically at local labour markets.[1]

---

1 Disability and related workers are those who are in the same four-digit occupational grouping as the 'Disability workers' and 'Aged and disabled care workers' listed earlier. As an example, rather than just including 'Disabilities services officers', the classification used in this part of the project includes all 'Welfare support workers' including 'Community workers', 'Family support workers,' 'Parole or probation officers', 'Residential care officers' and 'Youth worker.' We do this partly for data reasons (the publicly available data only has this level of disaggregation). However, this also serves a practical purpose as the NDIS is likely to use related occupations as well as encourage people to move from occupations with similar skill requirements into the disability workforce.

The first step in the analysis is to allocate these workers to a local labour market. We do this based on the Statistical Local Area (SLA) in which the individual identifies their place of work. In many cases, this is likely to be different to the area in which they live. We then compare this disability workforce to the number of people in the area, as well as the geographic size of the area. Results for this first part of the analysis are presented in Table 7.1, which gives the number of disability and related workers by remoteness, the number of disability and related workers per 100 000 persons, and the number of workers per square kilometre.

Table 7.1 Distribution of disability and related workers by remoteness area, Australia, 2006

Remoteness category	Number of workers	Workers per 100 000 population	Workers per km^2
Major cities	115 748	722	3.91816
Inner regional	40 579	958	0.11177
Outer regional	18 606	842	0.01832
Remote	3 132	884	0.00258
Very remote	3 087	1 629	0.00061
Australia	181 152	787	0.02352

Source: Customised calculations based on the 2006 Census of Population and Housing

Results presented in the first two columns of Table 7.2 correspond reasonably closely to those from AIHW (2009b) discussed earlier. The total number of disability and related workers decreases across the remoteness hierarchy, that is from 115 748 in 'major cities' to 3 087 in 'very remote' locations. However, per head of population, 'very remote' areas and, to a lesser extent, 'inner regional' areas have the greatest number of workers per 100 000 usual residents. The final columns show that in terms of geographic concentration, there are far more workers per square kilometre in major cities compared to very few workers in 'remote' and 'very remote' areas.

Although the final column of numbers hints at the much greater distance people living outside 'major cities' have to travel to access disability and related workers, there is significant geographic concentration in these areas of both population and workers. In order to capture this, we calculate the average number of disability and related workers per 100 000 usual residents as well as the number of workers per square kilometre in the SLA in which a person lives. This method takes into account the fact that although there are many SLAs with large areas and few workers, the majority of people (even in 'regional' and 'remote' areas) live in SLAs with much greater densities. It also allows us to calculate the average number of workers (per usual resident and per square kilometre) in the average area in which Indigenous Australians live compared to the average area in which non-Indigenous Australians live.[2]

Table 7.2 Average number of disability and related workers in the area by Indigenous status and remoteness area, Australia, 2006

Remoteness category	Average number of workers per 100 000 residents		Average number of workers per km^2	
	Indigenous	Non-Indigenous	Indigenous	Non-Indigenous
Major cities	800	722	12.43	14.17
Inner regional	1 175	953	2.52	2.41
Outer regional	1 032	831	3.44	2.23
Remote	1 538	794	1.14	1.36
Very remote	1 823	1 469	0.27	2.80
Australia	1 139	779	5.71	10.67

Source: Customised calculations based on the 2006 Census of Population and Housing

Results presented in Table 7.2 show that at the time of the 2006 Census the average Indigenous Australian had 1 139 disability and related workers per 100 000 usual residents in the area in which they lived. This was roughly 1.5 times as high as non-Indigenous Australians who were estimated to have 779 disability and related workers per 100 000 usual residents in the area in which they lived. Once again, though, the overall picture changes when looking at the number of workers per square kilometre. In 'major cities' there were on average 12.43 disability and related workers per square kilometre in the areas in which Indigenous Australians lived. This was slightly lower than the average for the 'major city' areas in which non-Indigenous Australians lived (14.17 workers per square kilometre). By comparison, there was greater access for Indigenous Australians in regional areas, and in particular 'outer regional' areas, compared to non-Indigenous Australians. It is in 'very remote' areas, however, where the difference is greatest.

There were about 111 000 non-Indigenous Australians counted in 'very remote' areas in the 2006 Census. On average, these non-Indigenous Australians had about 2.8 disability and related workers per square kilometre in the SLAs in which they lived. Compared to this, there were on average only 0.27 disability and related workers per square kilometre in the SLAs in which the estimated 78 000 'very remote' Indigenous Australians lived. Table 7.2 therefore demonstrates that across Australia there were on average almost twice as many disability and related workers per square kilometre in the areas in which non-

---

2   Similar to age standardisation of disease rates, geographic standardisation uses the proportion of the Indigenous population in each geographic region with a particular characteristic (in this case the SLA) as the basis of the calculations, but weights each region by the share of the non-Indigenous population in that region as opposed to the Indigenous population when calculating national percentages.

Indigenous Australians live compared to those in which Indigenous Australians live. So, although there are disability and related workers available, Indigenous Australians have to travel much greater distances to access them.

Indigenous Australians in the disability workforce

One of the key issues identified in this paper has been the importance of providing disability services in a culturally appropriate and competent way. While this need not always be done through an Indigenous workforce, Indigenous Australians are often well-suited to provide services in a way that Indigenous Australians themselves demand. Of the 455 028 people who identified as Indigenous in the 2006 Census, 9 467 were employed in the community services workforce, making up 3.2 per cent of total community service workers. This is not only higher than the 2.5 per cent Indigenous representation in the Australian population, but almost two-and-a-half times as high as the share of the total workforce (1.4%). Of those Indigenous Australians involved in the community services workforce, 5 247 or 55 per cent were involved either directly or indirectly in providing disability support services. The 2006 Census counted 425 disability workers, 1 792 disability or aged care workers, and 3 030 workers in other community services.

Between the 2001 and 2006 Censuses, the number of Indigenous workers in community services workers rose by 72.7 per cent. This is much faster than the growth in the community services sector as a whole, meaning that Indigenous representation in the sector increased from 2.5 per cent to 3.2 per cent. The largest increase was in other community services, which rose from 6.2 per cent to 9.2 per cent, while representation in disability and aged care increased slightly from 2 per cent to 2.2 per cent. The share of Indigenous people working as disability workers remained unchanged at 1.1 per cent.

Indigenous workers in the community services sector are younger on average than non-Indigenous workers in the sector. Around 40 per cent of Indigenous workers in the sector were younger than 35 in 2006, compared with 33 per cent of non-Indigenous workers. On the other hand, around 44 per cent of non-Indigenous workers were over 45 years of age, compared with only 30 per cent of Indigenous workers. The modal age group for non-Indigenous workers was 45–54 years, while for Indigenous workers it was 35–44 years. Over three-quarters (77.3%) of Indigenous workers in the community services sector were female. The proportion of female Indigenous workers is highest for the 15–24 years age bracket (84.5%) and lowest for the 55–64 years age bracket (72.3%).

Compared with other health services, Indigenous workers in the disability workforce tended to be employed for fewer hours. Disability workers and those employed in disability and aged care worked an average of 29 hours per week, while those employed in other community services worked on average 31 hours per week. This compares with an average of 35 hours for the health services industry as a whole, 33 hours for the community services sector, and 37 hours for all other occupations.

In all States and Territories the proportion of Indigenous workers in the disability workforce was higher than the Indigenous share of the total workforce. The relative proportion of Indigenous disability workers was highest in New South Wales (3.6% of disability workers compared to 1.2% of the workforce), Western Australia (5.3% compared with 1.7%), South Australia (2.9% compared with 0.9%) and the Northern Territory (35.2% compared with 13.4%). The representation of Indigenous workers in the disability sector was still high, but relatively less so, in Victoria (0.9% compared with 0.4%), Queensland (4% compared with 2.1%), Tasmania (3.7% compared with 2.6%) and the Australian Capital Territory (1.9% compared with 0.8%).

The relatively high rate of participation in community service occupations means that most Indigenous Australians live in areas with an Indigenous worker. Using the disability and related worker classification introduced earlier, there is on average 1 450 Indigenous workers per 100 000 Indigenous usual residents in the SLAs in which Indigenous Australians live. While access to an Indigenous disability workforce is somewhat lower in 'major cities' (1 197 Indigenous workers per 100 000 Indigenous usual residents), there were 1 719 and 1 857 workers in 'remote' and 'very remote' areas respectively. 'Inner regional' and 'outer regional' areas fall somewhere in-between (1 542 and 1 393 Indigenous workers respectively).

Indigenous carers as a potential workforce

Despite the currently high rate of Indigenous participation in the disability workforce, it is likely that the introduction of the NDIS will necessitate an expansion of the Indigenous workforce. A potential source of labour is the large number of informal carers currently supporting people with disabilities. Consider Table 7.3, which gives the proportion of Indigenous and non-Indigenous adults (by broad age group) that, according to the 2006 Census, provided unpaid assistance to a person with a disability.

Around 13.3 per cent of Indigenous adults provided unpaid assistance to a person with a disability. This rises to 16.0 per cent of the population aged 50–64 years. The rate of unpaid assistance is highest in very remote Australia with, somewhat surprisingly, relatively low rates in remote areas. Rates are also higher on average for Indigenous Australians compared to non-Indigenous Australians, driven mainly by higher levels of assistance provided by those aged 15–49 years.

Not only are Indigenous Australians more likely to be unpaid carers of someone with a disability than non-Indigenous Australians, those who are carers are much more likely to be doing so instead of paid employment. Around 46.1 per cent of all Indigenous carers aged 15–64 years were employed compared to 64.3 per cent of non-Indigenous carers in the same age group. This difference between the employment rates for Indigenous and non-Indigenous carers is even higher in remote and very remote Australia where 46.0 per cent and 49.6 per cent of Indigenous carers respectively are employed, compared to 70.3 per cent and 74.3 per cent for non-Indigenous carers. Similarly, there were slightly larger differences by Indigenous status for the relatively young (aged 15–49 years) compared to the relatively old (aged 50 years and over).

Table 7.3 Proportion of Indigenous and non-Indigenous Australians who provided unpaid assistance to a person with a disability, 2006

Remoteness category	Indigenous (%)			Non-Indigenous (%)		
	15–49 years	50–64 years	Total	15–49 years	50–64 years	Total
Major cities	12.4	17.1	13.1	8.8	16.9	10.9
Inner regional	13.0	17.2	13.6	10.0	17.4	12.3
Outer regional	12.4	15.2	12.8	9.5	15.5	11.4
Remote	11.3	12.9	11.6	7.7	12.2	9.0
Very remote	14.6	14.9	14.7	6.5	8.8	7.1
Total	12.8	16.0	13.3	9.1	16.8	11.2

Source: Customised calculations from the 2006 Census of Population and Housing

To the extent that this unpaid assistance is being provided due to a lack of alternative services, the NDIS provides an opportunity for the support that Indigenous carers provide to be appropriately recognised and rewarded as paid employment. Indeed in many more remote locations it is probable, and indeed appropriate, that the workforce for providing care services is drawn from the local community.

This will involve many challenges.

- There may need to be significant investments in the skills and qualifications of employed community members. This needs to address not just the specifics of care service provision but also the relatively low level of formal education among Indigenous carers, and in many cases a lack of experience in paid employment.

- In many communities the employment of community members as care service providers also raises issues of close kinship relationships. In some communities where separate Indigenous communities are co-located as a consequence of historical decisions, including forcible resettlements, there may be potential conflicts within a community.

- In small communities with limited infrastructure and often remote from oversight or competing service options, there are questions of how to develop and maintain appropriate service standards.

- In the Productivity Commission Report there was some discussion of the potential of paying close family members. We have discussed this issue in Chapter 1. However, the results presented in this section clearly demonstrate the need to consider a greater degree of flexibility in how these restrictions are applied, especially in a 'remote' and 'very remote' context where limited alternatives may exist.

One possible model is for close family members to be able to be employed, but via a third party. One option is to do this through the new Remote Jobs and Communities Program (the replacement for the CDEP scheme), where job seekers could be trained and placed in new employment opportunities created by the NDIS in remote locations (see Chapter 5; Department of Social Services 2013).

Developing approaches to these questions will require considerable effort. It is important that this process commences early and is undertaken in close consultation with people with a disability living in these communities, as well as with carers and others involved in providing services to them.

8. Key issues for disability service delivery models for remote Indigenous communities

The data and evidence provided and discussed in the earlier chapters have significant implications for the design of a disability service delivery model. Effective screening and assessment of disability will be paramount, and specific approaches are likely to be needed to address the nature of Indigenous disability. In terms of provision of disability services, issues include the training needs of a disability workforce, the extent to which disability support services should be built upon the health system, the implications of significantly higher rates of disability in the Indigenous population, and barriers to accessing services. These issues need to be considered together with the demographic and geographic characteristics of the Indigenous population to develop understanding of how the NDIS should be designed and, equally importantly, implemented.

Screening and assessment of disability

A crucial component which will be required for the successful implementation of the NDIS will be accurate and reliable identification of disability and, in particular, Tier 3 disability. While this is true for the Australian population as a whole, the challenges are likely to be particularly pronounced for the Indigenous population in general, and especially for the Indigenous population in remote and very remote areas. The Productivity Commission's (2011) model involves assessment being conducted by allied health professionals approved or appointed by the National Disability Insurance Agency and trained in the use of assessment tools. In the model, assessments would not be rubber-stamped and deviations of assessed needs outside the norms would require further investigation.

The nature of Indigenous disability is likely to require some specific approaches and strategies. In addition, it is likely that a tailored approach will be necessary in remote communities and perhaps to some extent in regional communities. First, the complex nature of Indigenous disability and the prevalence of dual diagnoses means that the screening for and assessment of disability in the Indigenous population will take additional time and probably require more specialist expertise. Second, the lack of confidence and the level of fear or distrust that some Indigenous people have towards services, particularly those funded or provided by government, means that it will be important to invest in community relations and building trust within the community. There is extensive practical experience and some research literature about how this can best be achieved.

It appears that in some communities the most effective model will be for local primary health care services to be funded to undertake the assessment. However, not all local primary health care teams are adequately skilled or resourced to undertake such assessments. As will be discussed below, this also raises issues around the fit between health and disability services. Many other communities will not possess the people with the skills required for the assessment of whether an individual meets the NDIS criteria. This means that either people with a disability will need to travel to a larger town for the assessment, or professionals with the requisite skills will be required to visit the communities. The medical model of outreach services which could be hub-and-spoke, visiting services, or fly-in fly-out services, may be appropriate. It appears that there will be some circumstances where technology-based models will be useful in the assessment process.

Provision of disability services

It is possible to think about disability services as falling into three types. The first is services that are associated with meeting the basic care needs of a person with a disability—that is, attendant care and community access. The second is early intervention services which aim to reduce the impact of disability and can cover such things as alleviating the impact of an existing disability or preventing the deterioration of an existing disability. Early intervention services may be provided when the disability is first identified, when there is a change in the disability, or at lifetime transition points. Examples of early intervention services are accommodation support; aids and appliances; behaviour and specialist interventions; case management, local coordination and development; and home and transport modifications. The third type of service is rehabilitation services.

In general, providing attendant care and community access does not require a high level of training, and workers providing this type of care are not highly paid. It is clear that one of the major issues for the success of the NDIS in remote areas is the ability to access a workforce. In the remote context the workforce for the provision of attendant care and community access will almost certainly need to come from within the community. As noted in Chapter 7 on workforce issues, in remote communities there is a large pool of potential workers, many of whom are already providing informal unpaid care (although they may be receiving an Australian government carer payment). There are several issues that will need to be considered here. In many communities the potential carer workforce will be related to the person with a disability. Consideration must be given as to how to provide basic training and ensure that the work environment for carers is safe. It will be necessary to ensure that the care that is paid for is adequate and periodically monitor the quality of care (as done in other countries like Germany) with consideration given to which organisation would formally employ the carers.

Given that many Indigenous people with a disability also have a range of health problems and that considerable activity has been undertaken in seeking to build an effective health care system in remote areas, a central question is the extent to which disability support services in remote areas should be built upon the health care system. Despite the need to integrate services delivered through the NDIS with the primary health care system, it is clear from the submissions made to the Productivity Commission and consultations undertaken for the research reported in this monograph, that some Indigenous people felt that the health model was not appropriate for providing disability services. This is due in part to the tendency of health services to not fully take into account the broader needs of people with a disability. For example, the submission by the FPDN (2011: 13) suggests that:

> Historically much of the focus on Aboriginal people with disability has been from a health perspective. Whilst this is essential, particularly regarding primary health interventions, it has come at the cost of failing to recognise the social aspects of disability. This has meant that the barriers that produce discrimination against Aboriginal people with disability remain firmly entrenched and the general well-being of Aboriginal people with disability has not improved in any meaningful way.

The social impact of Indigenous disabilities may well differ substantially from disabilities in non-Indigenous social contexts. Careful consideration needs to be given to how to ensure that the services provided are appropriate to the specific needs of people with a disability and are acceptable to them. This area requires further exploration, careful evaluation and monitoring.

Implications of high rates of disability

The NDIS will be particularly important for the Indigenous population given the relatively high rates of disability experienced by Indigenous people. The research reported in this monograph provides an overview of the some of the key issues related to the nature of Indigenous disability, and the types of services and models for the delivery of disability services which are most likely to meet the needs of the Indigenous population. Indigenous Australians experience profound or severe core activity limitations at more than double the rate of non-Indigenous Australians. This is in part due to socioeconomic disadvantage, and in part to a constellation of other risk factors such as lower rates of education, higher rates of smoking, substance abuse, and poor nutrition.

Not only are rates of disability higher for Indigenous Australians, they also face significant additional barriers to accessing disability planning and support services. In part this is due to a lack of disability services and disability-friendly housing and transport in remote areas. However, there are other demographic and geographic characteristics of the Indigenous population that are likely to impact on how the NDIS should be designed and implemented.

First, the Indigenous population is relatively young. This means that a relatively large proportion of the Indigenous population will be within the scope of the NDIS, as opposed to the aged-care system. Furthermore, the type of disabilities experienced by the Indigenous population will be different to those of the non-Indigenous population. The second demographic characteristic of relevance is that the Indigenous population is growing at a much faster rate than the non-Indigenous population, meaning that the Indigenous population will take on a greater share of services provided by the NDIS over the next few decades. Although all age groups of the Indigenous population are projected to grow over the next few decades, the Indigenous population is ageing and projected to age even faster over the next few decades. Like other populations, Indigenous Australians are shown to have higher levels of disability at older age groups. This means that regardless of any policy changes, the incidence of disability among the Indigenous population is projected to increase over the coming decades.

The Indigenous population is much more likely to live in remote and very remote Australia relative to the non-Indigenous population. In some of the larger remote communities, the introduction of the NDIS may lead to a significant inflow of funds as services that are currently being provided informally begin to be provided on a fee-for-service basis. However, many Indigenous people live in very small communities which in absolute terms will have very few people with a disability. This calls into question the ability of market mechanisms to meet the needs of the Indigenous population with a disability across remote Australia.

Despite this relative concentration in remote areas, the majority of Indigenous Australians still live in urban areas. Furthermore, the Indigenous population is projected to become increasingly urban over the next few decades. Although there are likely to be a range of services available to Indigenous Australians in urban areas, there are still a number of characteristics shared by Indigenous Australians across the country that will impact on the NDIS.

Indigenous people with a disability are relatively more likely to suffer from an intellectual disability than are non-Indigenous Australians. Related to this, there is a higher incidence of complex needs and issues which span health, disability and other aspects. An example is substance abuse combined with cognitive impairment. Furthermore, many Indigenous people with a disability are themselves caring for one or more other persons with a disability. A final issue that arose in consultations and a review of the literature is both a lack of awareness of disability among some groups of Indigenous Australians, and a reluctance of other Indigenous Australians with a disability to identify as such, either in survey data or to service providers.

The reluctance of some Indigenous Australians with a disability to identify as such is likely to make it more difficult to implement, monitor and evaluate the NDIS. The National Disability Insurance Agency will therefore need to raise awareness of disability issues in the Indigenous population. Service providers will also need to become more familiar with Indigenous-specific issues. Data collectors also have a responsibility to ensure that their collections give as accurate an account of Indigenous disability as possible.

We make a number of other specific recommendations for data collection. First, the Disability Module included in the NATSISS and GSS could be modified to correspond more closely with the SDAC. This will have a negative impact on data comparability, but given the importance of the NDIS as a policy initiative, this is a trade-off that may be worthwhile. In addition, the sample size for Indigenous Australians in the SDAC could be increased to enable reliable estimates for the Indigenous population at the national, State/Territory and remoteness levels.

A number of other changes could be made to the NATSISS. It could collect disability information for persons of all ages, not just those 15 years and over, and consider expanding the broader criteria to remote areas to address gaps in coverage. For future NATSISS surveys, 'Disability services' could be added as a specific category to the data item on types of services people have problems accessing in order to provide comparable data on the Indigenous population to that obtained for the total population from the GSS. Finally, there is a need to undertake work to examine methods to assess the level of Indigenous under-identification in DS NMDS data in order to gain a better understanding of the level of under-identification in this collection, as it is not currently known.

There is much that governments and other service providers can undertake do to maximise the chances of a successful implementation of the NDIS for Indigenous Australians. Issues related to the incorporation of the Indigenous population into the NDIS are summarised in Fig. 8.1 in order to highlight the interrelationships.

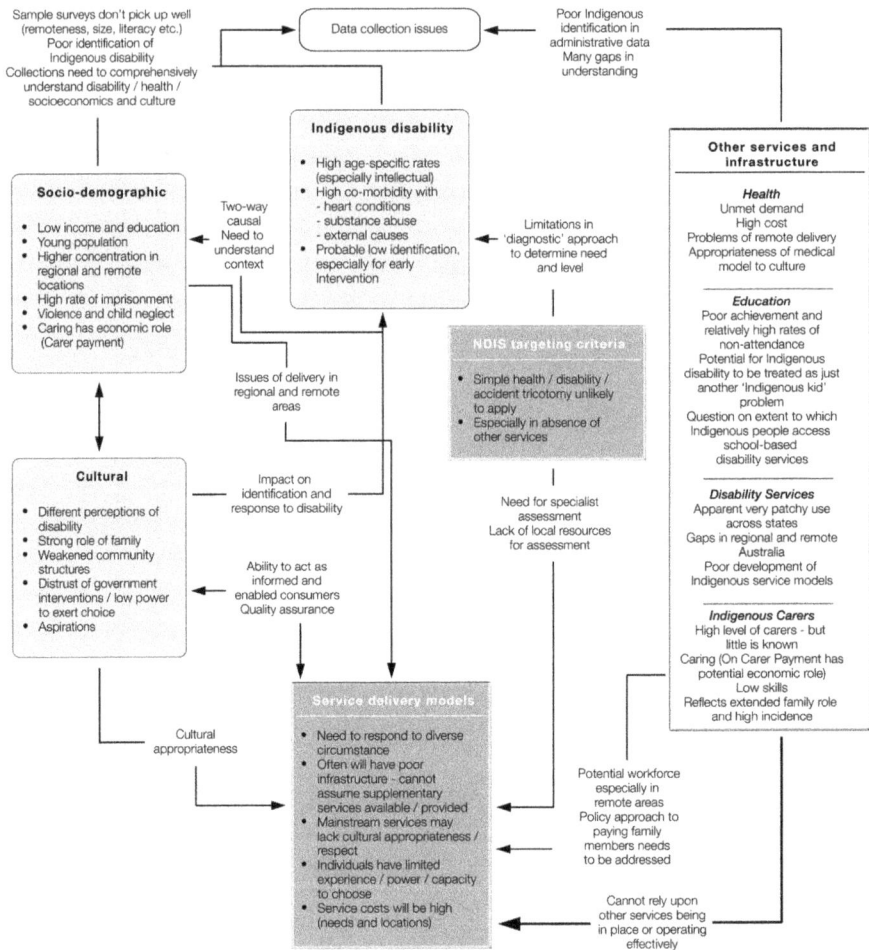

Fig. 8.1 Key issues for Indigenous Australians and the National Disability Insurance Scheme

Source: Authors' own conceptualisation

In many regional, rural and remote communities what is often needed are broad-based generalist services which will support the specialist services delivered through the NDIS. To the extent to which people with a disability will need to travel to larger towns for assessment or to access services, it will be important to consider access to transport needs alongside the provision of disability services. Another area which needs to be considered is the interaction between disability services provided through the NDIS and the criminal justice system.

While this is relevant to both the Indigenous and non-Indigenous population, it is particularly important for the Indigenous population, given the relatively high rates of incarceration of Indigenous Australians.

The NDIS presents an opportunity to improve the employment prospects and level of community infrastructure in remote and regional communities. As observed earlier, providing attendant care and community access does not generally require a high level of training. In the remote context the majority of the workforce for the provision of attendant care and community access will almost certainly need to come from within the community. As noted in Chapter 7, in remote communities there is a large pool of potential workers, many of whom are already providing informal care which is unpaid or remunerated through an Australian government carer payment.

Given that many Indigenous people with a disability also have a range of health problems and that the health care system in remote areas is in general far better developed than disability services, it seems likely that disability services in remote areas will need to be built upon the health care system. This would appear to differ from the general approach outlined in the Productivity Commission Report, which advocates a greater separation between disability and health services. This does not appear to be a feasible approach, given the difficulties of delivering services in remote areas and the relatively small number of people who are expected to be covered by the NDIS in most discrete Indigenous communities. Also, integrating disability and health services could address short-term disabilities (such as those experienced by people discharged from hospital into remote communities after surgery) as well as the long-term disabilities targeted by NDIS.

For reasons of scale, including accessing expensive and limited infrastructure in many communities, and for providing professional support and backup to service workers, the option of building disability services on the health care system is one which may need to be considered, especially where these community health services have developed strong community bonds. However, careful consideration would need to be given to the means of ensuring that the services which are provided are appropriate to the specific needs of people with a disability and are acceptable to them, that disability support does not follow a simple 'medical model', nor that inappropriate stress is placed on already stretched services which often cannot fully meet existing demand.

References

Aboriginal Disability Network New South Wales 2007. Telling It Like It Is: A Report on Consultations With Aboriginal People With Disability and Their Associates Throughout NSW, 2004–05, Aboriginal Disability Network of NSW, Strawberry Hills.

Ariotti, L. (1999) 'Social Construction of Anangu Disability', Australian Journal of Rural Health, 7 (4): 216–222.

Australian Bureau of Statistics (ABS) 2006. Census Dictionary, 2006 (Reissue), cat no. 2901.0, ABS, Canberra.

—— 2007. Population Distribution, Aboriginal and Torres Strait Islander Australians, cat. no. 4705.0, ABS, Canberra.

—— 2008a. Experimental Estimates of Aboriginal and Torres Strait Islander Australians, June 2006, cat. no. 3238.0.55.001, ABS, Canberra.

—— 2008b. Experimental Estimates of Aboriginal and Torres Strait Islander Australians (Indigenous Religions), cat. no. 3238055001DO002_200606, ABS, Canberra.

—— 2009a. Experimental Estimates and Projections, Aboriginal and Torres Strait Islander Australians, cat. no. 3238.0, ABS, Canberra.

—— 2009b. Experimental Life Tables for Aboriginal and Torres Strait Islander Australians, cat. no. 3202055003DO001_20052007, ABS, Canberra.

—— 2009c. 5–year Non Indigenous Life Tables, developed to be consistent with Cat. No. 3302055003DO001_20052007, ABS, Canberra.

—— 2010a. Disability, Ageing and Carers, Australia: Summary of Findings, cat no. 4430.0, ABS, Canberra.

—— 2010b. National Aboriginal and Torres Strait Islander Social Survey: User's Guide, 2008, cat no. 4720.0, ABS, Canberra.

—— 2010c. ABS Sources of Disability Information, Australia 2003–2006, cat. no. 4431.0.55.002, ABS, Canberra.

—— 2011. The Health and Welfare of Australia's Aboriginal and Torres Strait Islander Peoples 2010, cat no. 4704.0, ABS, Canberra.

—— 2012a. Australian Demographic Statistics, March 2012, cat no. 3101.0, ABS, Canberra.

—— 2012b. Births, Australia, 2011, cat. no. 3301.0, ABS, Canberra.

—— 2012c. Prisoners in Australia 2012, cat no. 4517.0, ABS, Canberra.

ABS & AIHW 2008. The Health and Welfare of Australia's Aboriginal and Torres Strait Islander peoples 2008, ABS & AIHW, Canberra.

Australian Institute of Health and Welfare (AIHW) 2009a. Australia's Welfare 2009, Australia's Welfare Series No. 9, cat. no. AUS 117, AIHW, Canberra.

—— 2009b. Health and Community Services Labour Force 2006, cat. no. IHW 43, AIHW, Canberra.

—— 2011a Aboriginal and Torres Strait Islander People with Disability, cat no. IHW 45, AIHW, Canberra.

—— 2011b. Disability Support Services 2009–10, AIHW, Canberra.

Australian National Audit Office (ANAO) 2012. National Partnerships Agreement on Remote Service Delivery, ANAO, Canberra.

Biddle, N. 2009. 'The geography and demography of Indigenous migration: Insights for policy and planning', CAEPR Working Paper No. 58, CAEPR, ANU, Canberra.

—— and Taylor, J. 2009. 'Indigenous population projections, 2006–31: Planning for growth', CAEPR Working Paper No. 56, CAEPR, ANU, Canberra.

Birks, M., Mills, J., Francis, K., Coyle, M., Davis, J. and Jones, J. 2010. 'Models of health service delivery in remote or isolated areas of Queensland: a multiple case study', Australian Journal of Advanced Nursing, 28 (1): 25–34.

Burton, J. 2012. Opening Doors through Partnerships: Practical Approaches to Developing Genuine Partnerships that Address Aboriginal and Torres Strait Islander Community Needs, Report to the Secretariat of National Aboriginal and Islander Child Care, North Fitzroy, viewed 3 September 2013, http://www.snaicc.org.au/_uploads/rsfil/02804.pdf.

Canadian Home Care Association 2010. Mind Body Spirit: Promising Practices in First Nations and Inuit Home and Community Care, viewed 3 September 2013, http://www.cdnhomecare.ca/media.php?mid=2343.

Commonwealth Grants Commission (CGC) 2012. Report on GST Revenue Sharing Relativities 2012 Update, CGC, Canberra.

Council of Australian Governments (COAG) 2008. Remote Service Delivery National Partnership Agreement, 4, COAG Fact Sheet, viewed 3 September 2013, http://www.coag.gov.au/node/262.

—— n.d. National Disability Agreement, viewed 22 October 2013, http://www.dhcs.act.gov.au/__data/assets/pdf_file/0019/103942/National_Disability_Agreement.pdf.

Department of Social Services (previously FaHCSIA) 2013. Remote Jobs and Communities Program (RJCP), viewed 4 November 2013, http://www.dss.gov.au/our-responsibilities/indigenous-australians/programs-services/communities-regions/community-development-employment-projects-cdep-program/remote-jobs-and-communities-program-rjcp.

Disability ACT 2011. Draft Policy Framework for Aboriginal and Torres Strait Islander People with a Disability and Their Families, Fact Sheet, viewed 4 November 2013, http://www.communityservices.act.gov.au/__data/assets/pdf_file/0004/186682/ATSI_Framework.pdf.

Disability Investment Group 2009. The Way Forward – A New Disability Policy Framework for Australia, viewed 3 September 2013, http://www.fahcsia.gov.au/sites/default/files/documents/05_2012/dig_report_19oct09.pdf .

Disability Services Queensland 2007. Growing Stronger: Investing in a better disability service system, Disability Services Queensland, viewed 4 November 2013, http://www.communities.qld.gov.au/resources/disability/publication/growing-stronger-summary.pdf.

Durst, D., Gay, A. and Morin, G. 2006. Urban Aboriginal Families of Children with Disabilities: Social Inclusion or Exclusion?, Research Project Report, Faculty of Social Work University of Regina, Regina, viewed 3 September 2013, http://www.fsin.com/healthandsocial/childportal/images/NAFC-Disability-17-03-06.pdf.

First Peoples Disability Network (FPDN) 2012. Final Submission to the Commission Inquiry into Disability Care and Support, viewed 27 November 2012, http://www.pc.gov.au/__data/assets/pdf_file/0012/110415/subdr1047.pdf.

Fisher, K., Gleeson, R., Edwards, R., Purcal, C., Siteki, T., Dinning, B., Laragy, C., D'Aegher, L. and Thompson, D. 2010. 'Effectiveness of individual funding approaches for disability support', Occasional Paper No. 29, FaHCSIA, Canberra.

Glasby, J. and Littlechild, R. 2009. Direct Payments and Personal Budgets: Putting Personalisation into Practice, The Policy Press, Bristol.

Health Canada 2008. Summative Evaluation of The First Nations and Inuit Home and Community Care, Report, Retrieved June 2012, viewed 27 November 2012, http://www.hc-sc.gc.ca/fniah-spnia/pubs/services/fnihcc-psdmcpni/index-eng.php.

Heard, G., Birrell, B. and Khoo, S-E. 2009. 'Intermarriage between Indigenous and non-Indigenous Australians', People and Place, 17 (1): 1–14.

Helps, Y. and Moller, J. 2007. Aboriginal People Travelling Well Literature Review: Driver Licensing Issues, Seat Restraint Non–compliance, Aboriginal Health, Aboriginal Disability, Australian Safety Transport Bureau, Canberra, viewed 3 September 2013, http://www.lowitja.org.au/sites/default/files/docs/Travelling-Well_lit-review_2007.pdf.

Holland, S., Pointon, K., & Ross, S. (2007). Who Returns to Prison?: Patterns of Recidivism Among Prisoners Released from Custody in Victoria in 2002-03. Research and Evaluation Unit, Corrections Victoria, Department of Justice.

House of Representatives Standing Committee on Family, Housing and Youth Affairs 2009. Who Cares...? Report on the Inquiry into Better Support for Carers, Parliament of the Commonwealth of Australia, Canberra, viewed 3 September 2013, http://www.aph.gov.au/parliamentary_business/committees/house_of_representatives_committees?url=fchy/carers/report.htm.

Humphreys, J. and Wakerman, J. 2008. Primary Health Care in Rural and Remote Australia: Achieving Equity of Access and Outcomes Through National Reform: A Discussion Paper, Report to National Health and Hospitals Reform Commission, viewed 3 September 2013, http://www.healthinfonet.ecu.edu.au/key-resources/bibliography?lid=16508.

Jenny Pearson & Associates Pty Ltd. 2009. Research of the Models of Advocacy Funded under the National Disability Advocacy Program, Report to FaHCSIA, Canberra, viewed 3 September 2013, http://www.fahcsia.gov.au/sites/default/files/documents/05_2012/rmaf_finalreport.pdf.

King, J. 2010. Weaving Yarns: The Lived Experience of Indigenous Australians with Adult-Onset Disability in Brisbane, PhD Thesis, Queensland University of Technology, Brisbane.

KPMG 2009. The Contemporary Disability Service System, Final Report, viewed 27 November 2012, http://www.dprwg.gov.au/sites/default/files/attachments/contemporary_disability_service_system_full_report.pdf.

Le Grand, J. 2007. The Other Invisible Hand: Delivering Public Services Through Choice and Competition, Princeton University Press, Princeton, New Jersey.

Mason, R. 2006. 'Providing social care services in rural Australia: A review', Rural Social Work and Community Practice, 11: 40–51.

National People with Disabilities and Carer Council 2009. SHUT OUT: The Experience of People with Disabilities and their Families in Australia, National Disability Consultation Report,, Canberra, viewed 3 September 2013, http://www.fahcsia.gov.au/our-responsibilities/disability-and-carers/publications-articles/policy-research/shut-out-the-experience-of-people-with-disabilities-and-their-families-in-australia.

NSW Ombudsman 2010. Improving Service Delivery to Aboriginal People with a Disability, A Review of the Implementation of ADHC's Aboriginal Policy Framework and Aboriginal Consultation Strategy, viewed 3 September 2013, http://www.ombo.nsw.gov.au/__data/assets/pdf_file/0011/3350/SR_ImprvServDeliAboriginalPeopDisability_Sept10.pdf.

Office of Evaluation and Audit (Indigenous Programs) 2009. Evaluation of Service Delivery in Remote Indigenous Communities, viewed 3 September 2013, http://www.anao.gov.au/uploads/documents/Evaluation_of_Service_Delivery_in_Remote_Indigenous_Communities.pdf.

Pawson, R. and Tilley, N. 2004. Realist Evaluation, Sage, London.

Productivity Commission 2011. Disability Care and Support, Report No. 54, Productivity Commission, Canberra.

Roufeil, L. and Battye, K. 2008. 'Effective regional, rural and remote family and relationships service delivery', AFRC Briefing No. 10, Australian Institute of Family Studies, Melbourne, viewed 3 September 2013, http://www.aifs.gov.au/afrc/pubs/briefing/b10pdf/b10.pdf.

Rural and Regional Health Australia 2012. The National Strategic Framework for Rural and Remote Health: Health Services, Rural and Regional Health Australia, Department of Health, viewed 27 November 2012, http://www.ruralhealthaustralia.gov.au/internet/rha/publishing.nsf/Content/NSFRRH~HealthServices.

Senior, K. 2000. Testing the ICIDH-2 With Indigenous Australians: Results of Field Work in Two Aboriginal Communities in the Northern Territory, Final

Report prepared for AIHW, ICIDH Collaborating Centre and the Department of Health and Family Services, viewed 27 November 2012, www.healthinfonet. ecu.edu.au/key-resources/bibliography/?lid=5812.

Steering Committee for the Review of Government Service Provision (SCRGSP) 2009. Report on Government Services 2009, Productivity Commission, Canberra, viewed 3 September 2013, http://www.pc.gov.au/gsp/rogs/2009.

—— 2011. Overcoming Indigenous Disadvantage: Key Indicators 2011, Productivity Commission, Canberra, viewed 3 September 2013, http://www. pc.gov.au/gsp/indigenous/key-indicators-2011.

Stopher, K. and D'Antoine, H. 2008. 'Aboriginal people with disability: Unique approaches to unique issues', Paper prepared for Disability Services Commission, Perth, viewed 27 November 2012, http://www.disability. wa.gov.au/dscwr/_assets/main/report/documents/doc/aboriginal.doc.

United Nations (UN) 2006. Convention on the Rights of Persons with Disabilities, viewed 4 September 2013, http://www.un.org/disabilities/default. asp?navid=14&pid=150.

Victorian Auditor-General's Office 2011. Individualised Funding for Disability Services, Victorian Auditor-General's Report 2011: 12–5, Melbourne, viewed 27 November 2012, http://www.audit.vic.gov.au/publications/20110914-Disability-Funding/20110914-Disability-Funding.pdf.

Vos, T., Barker, B., Begg, S., Stanley, L., & Lopez, A. D. (2009). Burden of disease and injury in Aboriginal and Torres Strait Islander Peoples: the Indigenous health gap. *International Journal of Epidemiology*, 38(2), 470-477.

Western Australia Disability Services Commission 2006. Aboriginal People with Disabilities: Getting Services Right, Booklet, viewed 4 September 2013, www.nds.org.au/asset/view_document/979317873.

Wilkes, E.T., Gray, D., Saggers, S., Casey, W. and Stearne, A. 2010. Substance misuse and mental health among Aboriginal Australians. In Purdie, N., Dudgeon, P. and Walker, R. (eds) *Working Together: Aboriginal and Torres Strait Islander Mental Health and Wellbeing Principles and Practice*. Australian Council for Educational Research, Canberra. pp. 117-134.

Appendix 1: Projection methodology for Remote Service Delivery Areas

Population projections: Overview

A variant of the standard Cohort Component Projection model is used for the projection of the Indigenous population of each Remote Service Delivery Area (RSDA). The necessary inputs to the model include hazard rates of births (fertility), deaths (mortality), and mobility (net migration). With estimates of projected fertility, mortality and migration, and base population estimates by five year increments in age for group and sex, the population of each region is projected over a 20-year period (2006–2026) using the standard cohort-component method. The population aged 5 years and over and the population aged under 5 years are calculated as follows:

$$A(r,g,x+5,y+5) \;=\; \left[A(r,g,x,y)\right]\left[s(r,g,x,y)\right]\left[1+m(r,g,x,y)\right], \; x \geq 0, \textit{(0)} \text{and}$$

$$A(r,g,0,y+5) = \frac{SR(g)}{2}\left\{ \begin{array}{l} \sum_{x=15}^{49}\left[b(r,x,y)A(r,f,x,y)\right]+ \\[2mm] \sum_{x=15}^{49}\left[b(r,x,y+5)A(r,f,x,y+5)\right] \end{array} \right\}\left[s(r,g,-5,y)\right]\left[m(r,g,-5,y)\right]$$

(0)

where

- $A(r,g,x,y)$ is the population in region r of sex g aged x in year y

- $A(r,f,x,y)$ is the female population in region r aged x in year y

- $b(r,x,y)$ is the fertility rate at age x in year y

- $m(r,g,x,y)$ is the migration ratio in region r for sex g; that is, the factor by which a cohort changes through migration in its transition from age x in year y to age $x+5$ in year $y+5$

- $s(r,g,x,y)$ is the mortality survival ratio in region r for sex g; that is, the probability that a person aged x in year y will survive to age $x+5$ in year $y+5$, and

- $SR(g)$ is the proportion of births that are of sex g.

The standard model above is altered to enable: (1) the inclusion of Indigenous and non-Indigenous births (see Chapter 1); and (2) the solving of a series of linear equations to estimate the effect of a 10 per cent diagonal migration scenario (see Chapter 1). This alteration to the standard model results in a simultaneous population projection of three populations. The first is the projection of the RSDA population of Indigenous persons only. The second is the projection of the RSDA population of non-Indigenous females only. The final comprises projections of survivors of the Indigenous population projections.

Four sets of scenarios are included in this modelling framework. Combining the migration, fertility and mortality scenarios leads to projection scenarios for each region shown in Table A1.1

Table A1.1 Indigenous population projection scenarios

Scenario ID	Migration	Fertility	Mortality
1	0	Constant	Constant
2	10% diagonal	Constant	Constant
3	0	25-year convergence	25-year convergence
4	10% diagonal	25-year convergence	25-year convergence

The remaining components of the projection methodology are outlined below.

Components of population change

Creating baseline Estimated Resident Population by sex by age by Indigenous status

As only total population counts are available, it is necessary to disaggregate these counts by age, sex and Indigenous status. Estimation of the age structure is imputed from ABS estimates of the age structure of the broader Indigenous region of which each RSDA is a member (ABS 2008a). A further complication is that Estimated Resident Population (ERP) counts by Indigenous Region (IREG) are upper censored to age 65+. To maintain the heterogeneity in the mortality estimates from the ABS Life Tables (ABS 2009b, 2009c), the upper censoring is split into 5-year age groups 65–85+ years. This is estimated using counts of Indigenous/non-Indigenous status by age at the relevant State level (ABS 2008b). ERP estimates are for June 2006.

Births

The projection of births by RSDA requires three separate estimates of fertility: (1) Indigenous births to Indigenous mothers; (2) Indigenous births to non-Indigenous mothers; and (3) non-Indigenous female births to non-Indigenous mothers. The final fertility estimate is necessary for female births only, as the

Indigenous projections only require the input of total births from the non-Indigenous population. An initial investigation was undertaken to see whether area-specific births data could be used to calculate the relevant fertility rates. Doing so resulted in too large a variation to be driven by fertility differences, and hence State-level births data was used for each of the three measures of fertility outlined above. To smooth out irregularities in the data, three year-averaged fertility rates are used based on data for 2005–2007. Two fertility assumptions were used in the projections. The first series keeps fertility rates (Indigenous and non-Indigenous) constant throughout the projection period. The second series results in a convergence of Indigenous and non-Indigenous fertility over a 25-year time frame. That is, the convergence occurs outside the projection period. The convergence results in the same fertility level (Total Fertility Rate) and well as fertility probability distribution (Age Specific Fertility Rates).

Deaths

State level Life Tables were used to calculate five-year survival ratios for both Indigenous and non-Indigenous populations (ABS 2009b, 2009c). For the projections, two scenarios are used: (1) Keeping non-Indigenous survival ratios at 2006 levels over the full projection period; and (2) converging the age-specific survival ratios of Indigenous and non-Indigenous persons over a 25-year period. The Indigenous survival ratios are increased linearly to the non-Indigenous rates over this time. That is, the average rate of change is constant over the projection period.

Migration

The final inputs required for the projection are estimates of migration, both in terms of level and age distribution. Two migration scenarios are used in the projections. The first sets net migration to zero for both the Indigenous and non-Indigenous population projections. The second assumption is more complicated, and is set out below.

This assumption results in a 10 per cent diagonal increase in the Indigenous population of each age cohort (excluding births), above that which would have been achieved with zero migration. As an example, Table A1.2 displays two age groups, 5–9 and 10–14 in 2006 and 2011. The ratio B/A represents the survival of the 5–9 cohort to 10–14 years in 2011, assuming no migration. To calculate the migration assumption, B/A is increased by 10 per cent (i.e. B/A + 0.1). An iterative linear search algorithm is then used to estimate the level of migration (net of survival) necessary to increase the 2011 population aged 10–14 by approximately 10 per cent. This approach has the advantage of imputing both an age structure of migration and an absolute level of migration.

This is particularly pertinent given the poor data quality at the RSDA level. The estimated migrants are projected as a subset of the population for future years, subject to both population decline through survival and population increase through fertility.

Table A1.2 Example migration table

	2006	2011
5–9	A	
10–14		B

Summary of results

The projection results are summarised by grouping all ages together in Tables A1.3, A1.4 and A1.5. In Table A1.3, the estimated non-Indigenous population in 2006 is given, as well as a projected population in 2026, calculated by applying the non-Indigenous annualised growth rate of 0.96 per cent per annum from Biddle and Taylor (2009). These are presented alongside the estimated Indigenous population in 2006 as well as the projected Indigenous population in 2026 for each of the four scenarios.

In Table A1.4, these population estimates/projections are used to calculate a projected annualised growth rate between 2006 and 2026. These are presented alongside the projected growth rates between 2006 and 2026 for the Indigenous Region that the community is located in, based on the zero migration scenario in Biddle and Taylor (2009). The main point to note in Table A1.4 is that in the absence of migration, all communities have a projected growth rate that is less than that for the region as a whole. This is driven mainly by the higher levels of births of Indigenous children to non-Indigenous mothers in the less remote parts of the regions which, demographically, dominate the results for the region as a whole. It is important to note, however, that the projected growth rates in the RSDAs are comparable to those for remote and very remote Australia in Biddle and Taylor (2009)—1.74 and 1.63 per cent per annum respectively—and larger than the non-Indigenous growth rate (0.96).

The proportion (percentage) of the population in the area estimated/projected to be Indigenous in 2006 and 2026 is given in Table A1.5.

Table A1.3 Estimated/projected non-Indigenous and Indigenous population in 2006 and 2026 by RSDA

Region Name	Non-Indigenous		Indigenous				
	2006	2026	2006	2026-S1	2026-S2	2026-S3	2026-S4
Amata	29	35	341	462	663	455	657
Angurugu	33	40	1 013	1 372	1 972	1 356	1 958
Ardyaloon	31	38	243	328	470	324	467
Aurukun	70	85	1 059	1 451	2 081	1 423	2 051
Beagle Bay	24	29	238	320	459	317	456
Coen	60	73	239	330	473	324	466
Doomadgee	61	74	1 102	1 546	2 211	1 507	2 168
Fitzroy Crossing	444	537	733	1 028	1 467	1 014	1 454
Galiwinku	147	178	2 158	2 930	4 208	2 895	4 178
Gapuwiyak	52	63	1 208	1 637	2 352	1 618	2 336
Gunbalanya	88	107	1 141	1 584	2 271	1 556	2 243
Halls Creek	261	316	1 092	1 515	2 168	1 492	2 145
Hermannsburg	68	82	938	1 261	1 811	1 246	1 798
Hope Vale	45	54	797	1 092	1 565	1 071	1 543
Lajamanu	105	127	735	1 010	1 446	991	1 427
Maningrida	176	213	2 600	3 610	5 174	3 545	5 111
Milingimbi	49	59	1 086	1 506	2 159	1 479	2 132
Mimili	36	44	289	393	563	387	558
Mornington Island	94	114	1 028	1 446	2 067	1 409	2 026
Mossman Gorge	0	0	165	233	333	227	327
Nguiu	85	103	1 463	2 031	2 911	1 994	2 875
Ngukurr	73	88	1 055	1 446	2 072	1 418	2 043
Numbulwar	64	77	713	968	1 391	957	1 381
Umbakumba	21	25	434	589	845	582	839
Wadeye	146	177	2 074	2 880	4 128	2 828	4 077
Walgett	1 002	1 213	1 220	1 748	2 488	1 696	2 429
Wilcania	154	186	453	637	910	618	888
Yirrkala	212	257	1 472	2 005	2 877	1 981	2 857
Yuendumu	92	111	701	946	1 358	935	1 348

Source: Authors' own calculation; Biddle & Taylor 2009

Table A1.4 Projected annual Australian Indigenous growth rates between 2006 and 2026 by RSDA and IREG

Region name	Remote Service Delivery Area				Indigenous Region	
	Scenario 1	Scenario 2	Scenario 3	Scenario 4	Name	Growth rate
Amata	1.53	3.38	1.45	3.33	Port Augusta	1.75
Angurugu	1.53	3.39	1.47	3.35	Nhulunbuy	1.69
Ardyaloon	1.51	3.35	1.45	3.32	Broome	1.82
Aurukun	1.59	3.43	1.49	3.36	Cape York	1.79
Beagle Bay	1.50	3.35	1.44	3.32	Broome	1.82
Coen	1.63	3.46	1.53	3.39	Cape York	1.79
Doomadgee	1.71	3.54	1.58	3.44	Mt Isa	1.93
Fitzroy Crossing	1.71	3.53	1.63	3.48	Derby	1.89
Galiwinku	1.54	3.39	1.48	3.36	Nhulunbuy	1.69
Gapuwiyak	1.53	3.39	1.47	3.35	Nhulunbuy	1.69
Gunbalanya	1.66	3.50	1.56	3.44	Jabiru	1.79
Halls Creek	1.65	3.49	1.57	3.43	Kununurra	1.92
Hermannsburg	1.49	3.34	1.43	3.30	Apatula	1.63
Hope Vale	1.59	3.43	1.49	3.36	Cape York	1.79
Lajamanu	1.61	3.45	1.51	3.38	Katherine	1.76
Maningrida	1.65	3.50	1.56	3.44	Jabiru	1.79
Milingimbi	1.65	3.50	1.56	3.43	Jabiru	1.79
Mimili	1.54	3.39	1.46	3.34	Port Augusta	1.75
Mornington Island	1.72	3.55	1.59	3.45	Mt Isa	1.93
Mossman Gorge	1.72	3.56	1.59	3.46	Cairns	2.03
Nguiu	1.65	3.50	1.56	3.44	Jabiru	1.79
Ngukurr	1.59	3.43	1.49	3.36	Katherine	1.76
Numbulwar	1.54	3.40	1.48	3.36	Nhulunbuy	1.69
Umbakumba	1.53	3.39	1.47	3.35	Nhulunbuy	1.69
Wadeye	1.65	3.50	1.56	3.44	Jabiru	1.79
Walgett	1.81	3.63	1.66	3.50	Bourke	1.58
Wilcania	1.72	3.55	1.56	3.42	Bourke	1.58
Yirrkala	1.56	3.41	1.50	3.37	Nhulunbuy	1.69
Yuendumu	1.51	3.36	1.45	3.32	Apatula	1.63

Source: Authors' own calculation; Biddle & Taylor 2009

Table A1.5 Proportion of Australian population estimated/projected to identify as Indigenous in 2006 and 2026 by RSDA

	2006	2026–S1	2026–S2	2026–S3	2026–S4
Amata	92.2	92.9	95.0	92.8	94.9
Angurugu	96.8	97.2	98.0	97.1	98.0
Ardyaloon	88.7	89.7	92.6	89.6	92.6
Aurukun	93.8	94.5	96.1	94.4	96.0
Beagle Bay	90.8	91.7	94.0	91.6	94.0
Coen	80.0	82.0	86.7	81.7	86.5
Doomadgee	94.8	95.4	96.8	95.3	96.7
Fitzroy Crossing	62.3	65.7	73.2	65.3	73.0
Galiwinku	93.6	94.3	95.9	94.2	95.9
Gapuwiyak	95.9	96.3	97.4	96.3	97.4
Gunbalanya	92.8	93.7	95.5	93.6	95.5
Halls Creek	80.7	82.7	87.3	82.5	87.2
Hermannsburg	93.2	93.9	95.7	93.8	95.6
Hope Vale	94.7	95.2	96.6	95.2	96.6
Lajamanu	87.5	88.8	91.9	88.6	91.8
Maningrida	93.7	94.4	96.0	94.3	96.0
Milingimbi	95.7	96.2	97.3	96.1	97.3
Mimili	88.9	90.0	92.8	89.9	92.8
Mornington Island	91.6	92.7	94.8	92.5	94.7
Mossman Gorge	100.0	100.0	100.0	100.0	100.0
Nguiu	94.5	95.2	96.6	95.1	96.5
Ngukurr	93.5	94.2	95.9	94.1	95.9
Numbulwar	91.8	92.6	94.7	92.5	94.7
Umbakumba	95.4	95.9	97.1	95.8	97.1
Wadeye	93.4	94.2	95.9	94.1	95.8
Walgett	54.9	59.0	67.2	58.3	66.7
Wilcania	74.6	77.4	83.0	76.8	82.7
Yirrkala	87.4	88.7	91.8	88.5	91.8
Yuendumu	88.4	89.5	92.4	89.4	92.4

Source: Authors' own calculation; Biddle & Taylor 2009

Appendix 2: How Indigenous persons with a disability were identified in the NATSISS, Census and SDAC

National Aboriginal or Torres Strait Islander Social Survey 2008

Data for the 2008 National Aboriginal and Torres Strait Islander Social Survey (NATSISS) were collected from Indigenous persons aged 15 years+ who were asked about the presence of disabilities or long-term health conditions which limited, restricted or impaired everyday activities, and lasted, or were expected to last for six months. People with a condition or long-term health condition in non-remote areas were identified using a broad set of criteria which included sensory, physical and learning difficulties, disfigurements and deformities, conditions which restrict physical activity or physical work, and mental illness for which supervision is required. More than one response could be provided. People residing in remote areas were also identified using these criteria. However, this measure did not include mental illness. People who reported at least one condition which lasted or was expected to last six months or more were also asked to nominate from a provided list of categories which restrictions they have experienced as a result of the reported condition(s). Data were also collected on assistance or supervision required for personal needs, moving around and talking with people. The wording of questions differed slightly between non-remote and remote areas, although this did not affect the underlying purpose of the questions being asked.

Responses provided data on what type of conditions, whether the conditions restricted everyday activities, and whether assistance or supervision were required to complete tasks are used to categorise respondents' into three levels of Disability Status: profound or severe core-activity limitation, unspecified limitation or restriction, or no disability or long-term health condition. The severity of restriction is also measured for those categorised as having profound or severe core-activity limitation.

Disability Type is categorised according to responses on the following type of conditions and whether they restricted everyday activities:

- sight, hearing, speech
- physical

- intellectual

- psychological

- type not specified, or

- no disability or long-term health condition.

Disability Type categories are the same for non-remote and remote areas, although in non-remote areas where respondents reported mental illness, they were included in the psychological category. Responses provided on the types of conditions and whether the conditions restricted everyday activities are used to categorise individuals into the following Types of Restrictions (ABS 2010a):

- sight problems

- hearing problems

- speech problems

- blackouts, fits or loss of consciousness

- difficulty learning or understanding things

- limited use of arms or fingers

- difficulty gripping things

- limited use of legs or feet

- any condition that restricts physical activity or physical work

- any disfigurement of deformity

- shortness of breath or difficulty breathing

- chronic or recurring pain

- a nervous or emotional condition

- long-term effects as a result of head injury, stroke or other brain damage

- any other long-term condition that requires treatment or medication

- any other long-term condition such as arthritis, asthma, heart disease, Alzheimer's disease, dementia etc., or

- no disability or long term health condition.

Census 2006

The 2006 Census collected one data variable relating to disability, which measured the number of people with a profound or severe disability. For the purpose of the Census, profound or severe disability was defined as the need for help or assistance in one or more of three core activity areas of self-care, mobility and communication, because of a disability, long-term health condition (lasting six months or more), or old age.

Questions 20–22 of the 2006 Census measured whether or not a person needed assistance in any of these three core activity areas:

- Question 20: Does the person ever need someone to help with, or be with them, for self-care activities?

- Question 21: Does the person ever need someone to help with, or be with them, for body movement activities?

- Question 22: Does the person ever need someone to help with, or be with them, for communication activities?

To determine if a person's need for assistance as reported in Questions 20–22 is due to severe or profound disability, Question 23 asks: 'What are the reasons for the need for assistance or supervision shown in questions 20, 21 and 22?'. The person is coded as 'Does not have need for assistance with core activities' if the response to question 23 is one or more of the following:

- no need for help or supervision

- short-term health condition (lasting less than six months)

- difficulty with English language

- other cause.

A person is coded as 'Has need for assistance with core activities' if the response to Question 23 is either one of the following:

- long-term health condition (lasting six months or more)

- disability (lasting six months or more).

If the response is 'old or young age' and the person is over 40 years old, then they are also categorised as having a need for assistance with core activities.

If the responses do not meet the requirements for needing or not needing assistance with core activities, the response can be coded as 'Not stated.' (ABS 2006).

Survey of Disability, Ageing and Carers 2009

For the purposes of the Survey of Disability, Ageing and Carers (SDAC), disability is defined as any limitation, restriction or impairment which restricts everyday activities and has lasted or is likely to last for at least six months. It includes difficulties with sight, hearing, speech and breathing. Chronic or recurrent pain, blackouts, fits, and learning difficulties are also included, as well as emotional or nervous conditions, physical conditions, disfigurement or deformity, mental illness, head injury, stroke and brain damage.

A series of screening questions are used to establish whether or not any members of a household may experience a disability. Where a member of a household meets the SDAC definition of disability, seven criteria are used to determine the severity of the disability, with the use of prompt cards describing everyday activities. The seven criteria are:

- if the person has a condition, impairment, limitation or restriction

- if the person always needs help or supervision with tasks

- if the person ever needs help or supervision

- if the person ever has difficulty with tasks

- if the person uses aids to assist with tasks

- if the person is 5–20 years of age and has an education restriction (the age range may vary according to the scope of the collection)

- if the person is aged less than 65 years and has an employment restriction.

Severity of disability is classified using seven base-level categories to determine Disability Status (ABS 2010b):

- profound core activity limitation

- severe core activity limitation

- moderate core activity limitation

- mild core activity limitation

- education/employment restriction only

- no specific limitation or restriction

- no disability or long-term health condition.

Disabilities can be broadly grouped depending on whether they relate to functioning of the mind or the senses, or to anatomy or physiology.

Each disability group may refer to a single disability or be composed of a number of broadly similar disabilities. The SDAC module relating to disability groups was designed to identify four separate groups based on the particular type of disability identified. These groups are:

Sensory

- loss of sight (not corrected by glasses or contact lenses)
- loss of hearing where communication is restricted, or an aid used
- speech difficulties, including loss.

Intellectual

- difficulty learning or understanding things.

Physical

- shortness of breath or breathing difficulties that restrict everyday activities
- blackouts, fits or loss of consciousness
- chronic or recurrent pain or discomfort that restricts everyday activities
- incomplete use of arms or fingers
- difficulty gripping or holding things
- incomplete use of feet or legs
- restriction in physical activities or in doing physical work
- disfigurement or deformity.

Psychological

- nervous or emotional condition that restricts everyday activities
- mental illness or condition requiring help or supervision
- head injury, stroke or other brain damage, with long-term effects that restrict everyday activity.

To identify whether a person has a particular type of limitation or restriction, the SDAC collects information on need for assistance, difficulty experienced, or use of aids or equipment to perform selected tasks. The tasks associated with each type of limitation and restriction are given in Table A2.1 (ABS 2010a).

Table A2.1 Tasks associated with limitation typing, SDAC

Limitation or restriction	Activity	Tasks
Specific limitation or restriction		
Core-activity limitations	Communication	Understanding family or friends
		Being understood by family or friends
		Understanding strangers
		Being understood by strangers
	Mobility	Getting into or out of a bed or chair
		Moving about usual place of residence
		Moving about a place away from usual residence
		Walking 200 metres
		Walking up and down stairs without a handrail
		Bending and picking up an object from the floor
		Using public transport
	Self care	Showering or bathing
		Dressing
		Eating
		Toileting
		Bladder or bowel control
Limitation or restriction	Activity	Tasks
Specific limitation or restriction		
Schooling or employment restrictions	Schooling	Unable to attend school
		Attends a special school
		Attends special classes at an ordinary school
		Needs at least one day a week off school on average
		Has difficulty at school
	Employment	Permanently unable to work
		Restricted in the type of work they can or could do
		Need, or would need, at least one day a week off work on average
		Restricted in the number of hours they can, or could, work
		Requires special equipment or modified work environment
		Needs ongoing assistance or supervision
		Would find it difficult to change jobs or get a preferred job
		Needs assistance from a disability job placement program or agency
Without specific limitation or restriction		
Other activities	Health care	Foot care
		Taking medications or administering injections
		Dressing wounds
		Using medical machinery
		Manipulating muscles or limbs

Paperwork	Reading or writing tasks such as:
	Checking bills or bank statements
	Writing letters
	Filling in forms
Transport	Going to places away from the usual place of residence
Housework	Household chores such as:
	Washing
	Vacuuming
	Dusting
Property maintenance	Changing light bulbs, taps, washers or car registration stickers
	Making minor home repairs
	Mowing lawns, watering, pruning shrubs, light weeding or planting
	Removing rubbish
Meal preparation	Preparing ingredients
	Cooking food
Cognition or emotion	Making friendships, interacting with others or maintaining relationships
	Coping with feelings or emotions
	Decision making or thinking through problems

Source: ABS (2010a)

Appendix 3: Key questions to inform NDIS and mapping to available data

Table A3.1 Key questions to inform NDIS and mapping to available data

Key questions – data capture	Data sources	Notes
(a) How many Indigenous Australians have a disability or limited core functioning? (b) What types of disability are they affected by? (c) What is the impact of the disability on their day-to-day functioning?	(a) NATSISS, Census (b) NATSISS (c) SDAC, NATSISS	1. Census data can be used to provide estimates of the total number of Indigenous people with disability (all ages) and comparisons to the non-Indigenous population. 2. Census and NATSISS data can be compared to provide estimates for Indigenous persons aged 15 years and over. 3. NATSISS data can be used to provide data on types of disability and impact on day-to-day functioning. 4. SDAC contains impact measures, however the Indigenous sample size will not enable reliable estimates to be produced (it is also not included on the CURF). NATSISS data on type of restriction could be used to give some indication of impact on day-to-day functioning, such as difficulty gripping things, difficulty understanding things, etc. 5. NATSIHS collects data on long-term health conditions but does not enable persons with a disability to be separated from persons without a disability who report a long-term condition. Therefore this data is not particularly useful.
What is the prevalence of disability in Indigenous communities by age band cohort?	NATSISS Census	1. Census data can be used to provide estimates for all age groups and to compare to the non-Indigenous population. 2. NATSISS data can be used to provide more detailed information on disability for Indigenous persons aged 15 years and over by age group e.g. by type of disability.
Where do Indigenous Australians with a disability live and what percentage lives in urban, regional or remote locations?	NATSISS Census	1. Census data can be used to report information at low-level geographies (e.g. Statistical Division and State/Territory by ASGC), and to compare Indigenous and non-Indigenous populations. 2. NATSISS data can be used to report information at the State/Territory and remoteness (ASGC) level for Indigenous Australians.
(a) What type of assistance is currently provided? (b) What are the outcomes?	a) DS NMDS b) Not available	1. DS NMDS data can be used to report information on types of assistance provided to Indigenous persons with a disability. Whether the main types of assistance provided differs by State/Territory, remoteness and age can be examined. 2. DS NMDS does not currently include data items on the outcomes of assistance provided/services received (such items are proposed for inclusion as part of a redevelopment of the NMDS for future collection). NATSISS/Census data could be reported to provide information on SES outcomes of persons with a disability.
What are the barriers that Indigenous Australians face in accessing community services generally and, more specifically, disability support services?	NATSISS, NATSIHS	1. NATSISS data can be used to report data on barriers to accessing services in general by type of service; however, it does not specify community or disability services as types of services. 2. NATSIHS data can be used to report data on barriers to accessing health services.

Appendix 4: Data sources on disability for the Indigenous population

Table A4.1 Data sources on disability for the Indigenous population: Scope, definitions, data items and data quality/gaps

Data source	Scope/ population	Time period/ frequency of collection	Definition of disability used	Disability data items of relevance	Geographical variables included in data set	Data quality/ data gaps
NATSISS	Indigenous people aged 15 years and over.	Every 6 years; last survey conducted in 2008	Disability or long-term health condition: person has one or more conditions which have lasted, or are likely to last, for six months or more, and that restrict everyday activities. Profound or severe core-activity limitation: person requires help or supervision for one or more core activities, such as self-care, mobility or communication.	Disability status: Profound or severe core-activity limitation Unspecified limitation or restriction Total with disability or long-term health condition Disability type: Sight, hearing speech Physical Intellectual Psychological Type of restrictions Sight problems Hearing problems Speech problems Blackouts, fits or loss of consciousness Difficulty learning or understanding things Limited use of arms or fingers Difficulty gripping things Limited use of legs or feet Any condition that restricts physical activity or physical work Any disfigurement or deformity Shortness of breath, or difficulty breathing Chronic or recurring pain A nervous or emotional condition Long term effects as a result of a head injury, stroke or other brain damage	State/Territory Remoteness (ASGC) State/Territory by ASGC (selected cross-classifications where sample size permits)	Detailed disability data only collected in non-remote areas: Additional criteria were used to identify people with disability in remote areas, meaning that the common criteria (remote + non-remote) is not strictly comparable between the 2002 and the 2008 surveys, or with non-Indigenous. As a result, analysis of comparisons with the 2002 NATSISS and with non-Indigenous Australians are restricted to persons living in non-remote areas only (using the broader criteria). Disability data items only collected for persons aged 15 years and over. Survey only conducted every six years. Non-Indigenous comparisons available from 2007–08 NHS and 2006 GSS.

151

Data source	Scope/population	Time period/ frequency of collection	Definition of disability used	Disability data items of relevance	Geographical variables included in data set	Data quality/ data gaps
				Any other long-term condition that requires treatment or medication Any other long-term condition. Whether has education restriction due to disability, and type of employment restriction. Whether has employment restriction due to disability, and type of education restriction		
Census	Total Australian population	5 yearly 2006 most recent data available. 2011 will be available in late 2012	Core activity need for assistance.	Disability status: Has core activity need for assistance Does not have core activity need for assistance	State/Territory Remoteness (ASGC) SLA SDD SD Postcode State/Territory by ASGC	Disability question included for first time in 2006 Census, so no time series. Census does not include questions on type of disability or impact measures. Census only conducted every five years.
SDAC	Total Australian population	6 yearly 2009 most recent.	Any limitation, restriction or impairment which restricts everyday activities and has lasted or is likely to last for at least six months. This definition includes a range of conditions that result in mild to profound limitations.	Disability status: Has disability and profoundly limited in core activities Has disability and severely limited in core activities Has disability and moderately limited in core activities Has disability and mildly limited in core activities Has disability and not limited in core activities but restricted in schooling or employment Has disability and not limited in core activities or restricted in schooling or employment Has a long-term health condition without disability No long-term health condition	State/Territory Remoteness (ASGC)	Indigenous sample size very small and data not considered to be reliable for reporting (Indigenous data item not included on CURF). Does not include very remote areas. Survey only conducted every six years.

Data source	Scope/ population	Time period/ frequency of collection	Definition of disability used	Disability data items of relevance	Geographical variables included in data set	Data quality/ data gaps
			Data definitions align with the International Classification of Functioning, Disability and Health.	or disability Disability type Loss of sight Loss of hearing Speech difficulties Breathing difficulties Chronic or recurrent pain or discomfort Blackouts, fits or loss of consciousness Learning or understanding difficulties Incomplete use of arms or fingers Difficulty gripping or holding things Incomplete use of feet or legs Nervous or emotional condition Restricted in physical activities or work Disfigurement or deformity Mental illness Receiving treatment Other type of restriction Conditions Main condition causing disability Cause of main condition Impact measures: Level of assistance needed with day to day tasks (listed) because of disability Broad area of activity where assistance is required or difficulty is experienced Specific types of activity where assistance is required or difficulty is experienced		

Data source	Scope/ population	Time period/ frequency of collection	Definition of disability used	Disability data items of relevance	Geographical variables included in data set	Data quality/ data gaps
				Whether additional aids are needed Whether receives assistance (formal/informal) with broad area activity Frequency of need for assistance Whether needs more formal/ informal assistance		
NATSIHS	Indigenous population (all ages)	6 yearly 2004–05 most recent	Long-term health condition.	Whether has long-term health condition	State/Territory Remoteness (ASGC) State/Territory by ASGC (selected cross-classifications where sample size permits)	No specific data items for disability - survey is not able to distinguish between persons with a long term health condition without a disability. Survey only conducted every six years.

Disability services NMDS	Users of disability support services where funding has been provided by a government organisation operating under the NDA.	Annual. Most recent data available 2009–10	Need for assistance in nine activity areas (ICF compliant).	Total number of disability support service users.
				Disability group (primary and other significant):
				Type of assistance provided (high level categories):
				  Accommodation support
				  Community support
				  Community access
				  Respite
				  Employment
				Type of assistance provided (specific categories):
				  Support needed:
				  Activities of daily living
				  Activities of work, education and community living
				  Activities of independent living
				  Amount of assistance (hours)
					Client:
					State/Territory
					ASGC
					Postcode
					Provider:
					Postcode
					SLA
					Sector
						The DS NMDS does not currently contain data on outcomes of services received; however, the DS NMDS is currently being redeveloped and will include such information in the future.
						Potential population is defined as people aged under 65 years with profound or severe core activity limitation.

Appendix 5: Attachment tables

Table A5.1 Need for assistance with core activities by Aboriginal and Torres Strait Islander people: Rate compared to non-Indigenous Australians, 2006

Age group	Indigenous	Non-Indigenous	Rate ratio
0–14	2.3	1.7	1.3
15–24	2.4	1.6	1.7
25–34	2.7	1.5	2.1
35–44	4.7	2.0	2.6
45–54	8.2	2.9	2.9
55–64	14.2	5.7	2.8
65 or over	28.2	14.6	1.8

Source: AIHW analysis of 2006 Census data (unpublished); AIHW 2011b

Table A5.2 Statistical Divisions with the highest number and proportion of Indigenous persons needing assistance with core activities, Australia, 2006

Statistical Division	Core activity need for assistance (no.)	Statistical Division	Core activity need for assistance (%)
Sydney	2 175	Wimmera	7.6
Northern (Qld)	1 498	Barwon	6.6
Northern Territory–Balance	1 373	East Gippsland	6.6
Brisbane	1 328	Loddon	6.5
Far North (Qld)	982	Yorke and Lower North	6.4
Hunter	878	Ovens–Murray	6.4
Perth	827	Gippsland	6.4
Melbourne	715	Wide Bay–Burnett	6.3
Mid-North Coast (NSW)	667	West Moreton	6.2
Adelaide	649	Southern (Tas)	6.1
North Western (NSW)	613	Upper Great Southern	6.1
Wide Bay–Burnett	495	Greater Hobart	6.0
Kimberley	466	Western District	6.0
Illawarra	455	Hunter	6.0
South Eastern	443	Mid-North Coast	5.9

Source: AIHW analysis of 2006 Census data (unpublished)

Table A5.3 Indigenous persons with core-activity need for assistance, by State/Territory, Australia, 2006

	Indigenous		Non-Indigenous		
	No.	Age standardised proportion[a]	No.	Age standardised proportion[a]	Age standardised rate ratio
NSW	6 907	7.7	263 724	4.1	1.9
Vic	1 588	7.8	201 714	4.1	1.9
Qld	4 812	6.7	146 041	4	1.7
WA	2 278	7.5	64 471	3.6	2.1
SA	1 250	8.1	70 397	4.4	1.8
Tas	871	7.7	21 735	4.5	1.7
ACT	150	6.8	9 897	3.7	1.8
NT	1 750	7.2	2 795	3.3	2.2
Australia[b]	19 613	7.4	780 817	4.1	1.8

a. Age-standardised to the 2001 Australian standard population.

b. Australia total includes other Territories.

Source: ABS & AIHW analysis of 2006 Census data (AIHW 2011b)

Table A5.4 Need for assistance with core activities, by remoteness and Indigenous status, Australia, 2006

	Indigenous		Non-Indigenous		
	Number	Age standardised proportion[a]	Number	Age standardised proportion[a]	Age standardised rate ratio
Major cities	7 007	7.5	520 953	4	1.8
Inner regional	4 824	7.7	175 193	4.3	1.8
Outer regional	4 105	7.1	74 279	4.1	1.8
Remote	1 466	7.3	7 212	3.3	2.3
Very remote	2 127	6.7	1 711	2.7	2.5
Australia[b]	19 613	7.4	780 817	4.1	1.8

a. Age-standardised to the 2001 Australian standard population.

b. Australia total includes other Territories.

Source: ABS & AIHW analysis of 2006 Census data (AIHW 2011a)

Table A5.5 Proportions of people aged 15 years and over in non-remote areas, by disability type, age and Indigenous status, Australia, 2008

	Indigenous		Non-Indigenous		Rate ratio[a]
	Prop. (%)	RSE[c] (%)	Prop. (%)	RSE[c] (%)	
Sight, hearing, speech					
15–24 years	9.1	12.0	4.9	14.5	1.8
25–34 years	11.5	10.4	6.8	9.9	1.7
35–44 years	16.0	11.2	9.0	7.8	1.8
45–54 years	24.7	11.0	15.3	5.7	1.6
55 years and over[b]	28.4	9.1	30.7	2.3	0.9
AS[c] total with sight, hearing, speech disability	18.9	5.7	15.0	2.3	1.3
Physical					
15–24 years	19.4	8.2	14.2	6.3	1.4
25–34 years	26.1	7.8	18.3	5.0	1.4
35–44 years	35.1	6.4	23.6	4.3	1.5
45–54 years	48.8	6.1	28.2	4.2	1.7
55 years and over	60.4	4.7	43.1	2.3	1.4
AS[c] total with physical disability	40.1	3.5	27.2	1.7	1.5
Intellectual					
15–24 years	10.8	12.2	3.3	17.4	3.3
25–34 years	7.5	15.0	1.9	19.7	3.9
35–44 years	7.5	17.2	2.2	17.4	3.4
45–54 years	11.5	17.3	2.4	16.4	4.9
55 years and over	6.0	18.6	3.1	9.8	1.9
AS[c] total with intellectual disability	8.3	9.1	2.6	6.9	3.2
Psychological					
15–24 years	7.7	14.3	3.4	15.1	2.2
25–34 years	9.8	13.0	3.7	13.2	2.7
35–44 years	11.8	14.2	4.3	11.1	2.7
45–54 years	16.2	12.3	5.5	9.6	2.9
55 years and over	12.9	13.2	5.3	8.0	2.4
AS[c] total with psychological disability	11.8	7.2	4.5	5.3	2.6

	Indigenous		Non-Indigenous		Rate ratio[a]
	Prop. (%)	RSE[c] (%)	Prop. (%)	RSE[c] (%)	
Type not specified					
15–24 years	12.4	11.3	6.0	10.3	2.1
25–34 years	17.4	8.8	6.8	8.2	2.5
35–44 years	23.7	8.7	9.3	8.0	2.5
45–54 years	40.3	7.1	14.9	5.7	2.7
55 years and over	54.3	5.5	29.4	3.1	1.8
AS[c] total with disability type not specified	31.9	3.9	14.8	2.6	2.2
Total persons with one or more disability type					
15–24 years	37.5	5.5	22.1	5.1	1.7
25–34 years	43.4	5.0	28.2	4.0	1.5
35–44 years	50.9	4.6	33.7	3.6	1.5
45–54 years	66.2	3.9	42.4	3.0	1.6
55 years and over	77.8	2.9	61.8	1.5	1.3
AS total with one or more disability types	57.3	2.5	40.0	1.2	1.4
No disability or long term condition(s)					
15–24 years	62.5	3.3	77.9	1.4	0.8
25–34 years	56.6	3.8	71.8	1.6	0.8
35–44 years	49.1	4.7	66.3	1.8	0.7
45–54 years	33.8	7.6	57.6	2.2	0.6
55 years and over	22.2	10.3	38.2	2.5	0.6
AS total with no disability or long term condition(s)	42.7	2.6	60.0	0.8	0.7
All persons					
15–24 years	100.0	–	100.0	–	–
25–34 years	100.0	–	100.0	–	–
35–44 years	100.0	–	100.0	–	–
45–54 years	100.0	–	100.0	–	–
55 years and over	100.0	–	100.0	–	–
Total persons aged 15 and over	100.0	–	100.0	–	–

a. The rate ratio is calculated by dividing the rate for Indigenous people by the corresponding rate for non-Indigenous people.

b. Difference between 2008 Indigenous and non-Indigenous rate is not statistically significant.

c. Prop.= Proportion; AS= Age standardised; RSE= Relative standard error; – Nil or rounded to zero.

Source: ABS NATSISS 2008, ABS National Health Survey 2007–08 (SCRGSP 2011)

Table A5.6 Education or employment restriction due to disability, Indigenous persons age 15–64 years, Australia, 2008

	Non-remote		Remote		Total	
	No.	%	No.	%	No.	%
Education restriction						
Has an education restriction due to disability	6 733	5.8	833	2.3	7 567	5.0
Does not have an education restriction due to disability	108 736	94.2	34 965	97.7	143 701	95.0
Total with a disability	115 469	100.0	35 798	100.0	151 267	100.0
Employment restriction						
Has an employment restriction due to disability	19 280	16.7	5 307	14.8	24 587	16.3
Does not have an employment restriction due to disability	96 190	83.3	30 491	85.2	126 681	83.7
Total with a disability	115 469	100.0	35 798	100.0	151 267	100.0

Source: AIHW analysis of 2008 NATSISS (unpublished)

Table A5.7 Disability status by equivalised gross household income, Aboriginal and Torres Strait Islander people aged 15 years and over, Australia, 2008

	Has disability or long-term health condition[a] (%)	No disability or long-term health condition (%)
First quintile (lowest)	44.6	35.3
Second quintile	15.8	18.4
Third quintile	9.8	12.5
Fourth quintile	6.6	9.6
Fifth quintile (highest)	2.7	4.4

a. Total with a disability or long-term health condition as determined by the common (remote + non-remote) criteria.

Source: 2008 NATSISS (ABS 2011a)

Table A5.8 Highest school attainment, by disability and Indigenous status, age 18–64 years, Australia 2006 and 2008[a]

	Indigenous Australians (2008 NATSISS)		All Australians (2006 GSS)	
	Severe or profound core activity limitations (%)	No disability or long-term health condition (%)	Severe or profound core activity limitations (%)	No disability or long-term health condition (%)
Year 12	15.7	28.4	31	58
Year 10 and 11	39.4	47.7	37	34
Year 9 and below	44.9	23.9	32	8
Total (no.)	20 722	135 441	516 487	8 477 923

a. 2008 NATSISS and 2006 GSS excluded special dwellings where higher proportions of people with disability may be found and 2006 GSS excluded very remote and sparsely settled areas.

Source: AIHW analysis of 2008 NATSISS and 2006 GSS (AIHW 2011b)

Table A5.9 Indigenous Australians aged 18–64 years, reasons for not studying further in the previous 12 months although wanted to, by disability, 2008[a]

	People with severe or profound core activity limitations (%)	Per cent of people with no disability or long-term health condition (%)
Too much work or other work reason or no time	7.0	8.6
Personal caring or other family reasons	12.7	8.5
Course related reasons	2.6	3.2
Too expensive or financial reasons	5.3	5.0
Other	1.8	2.1
Total wanting to study further (%)	29.5	27.2
Total (no.)	20 722	135 441

a. 2008 NATSISS included remote, very remote and indigenous communities but excluded special dwellings where higher proportions of people with severe and profound disability may be found.

Source: AIHW 2011b

Table A5.10 Self-assessed health status, by disability status and Indigenous status, persons aged 18–64 years, Australia, 2006 and 2008

Self-assessed health status	Indigenous Australians[a] (2008 NATSISS)		All Australians[b] (2006 GSS)	
	Severe or profound core activity limitations	No disability or long-term health condition	Severe or profound core activity limitations	No disability or long-term health condition
Excellent, very good, good	40.9	92.5	44.9	97
Fair, poor	59.1	7.5	55.1	3
Total number	20 722	135 441	516 487	8 477 923

a. 2008 NATSISS included remote, very remote and Indigenous communities but excluded special dwellings where higher proportions of people with severe and profound disability may be found.

b. 2006 GSS collected data on self-assessed health status from 18 years onwards, while 2008 NATSISS collected data on self-assessed health status from 0 years onward, 0–14 years by proxy. Data is presented in this table from 18–64 years for consistency.

Source: AIHW analysis of ABS NATSISS (AIHW 2011b)

Table A5.11 Number of stressors experienced in the previous 12 months by disability, Indigenous Australians aged 15–64 years, 2008[a]

Number of stressors[b]	Severe/profound core activity limitations		No disability or long-term health condition	
	No.	%	No.	%
nil stressors	5 127	23.3	80 286	49.9
1–2 stressors	10, 785	49	61 988	38.5
3–5 stressors	4 852	22	15 956	9.9
>5 stressors	1 216	5.5	2 652	1.7
not applicable			108	0.1
Total	22 015	100	147 758	100

a. 2008 NATSISS included remote, very remote and indigenous communities but excluded special dwellings where higher proportions of people with severe and profound disability may be found.

b. Stressors include 'really bad illness', 'really bad accident', mental illness, 'really bad disability', marriage, pregnancy, new family member, overcrowding at home, getting back together with spouse, divorce or separation, death, unable to get a job, lost job, changed jobs, pressure to fulfil cultural responsibilities, alcohol related problems, drug related problems, gambling problems, witness to violence, abuse or violent crime, self, family member, friend spent time in gaol, trouble with police, treated badly/discrimination, unwelcome at child's school (ABS 2010b).

Source: AIHW 2011b

Table A5.12 Indigenous disability support services users, all ages, States and Territories, Australia, 2005–06 to 2009–10

Year	NSW No.	Vic No.	Qld No.	WA No.	SA No.	Tas No.	ACT No.	NT No.	Australia No.
2005–06	1 709	1 795	1 433	1 045	634	168	42	410	7 182
2006–07	2 129	2 154	1 568	1 483	695	165	61	525	8 735
2007–08	2 882	2 323	2 143	1 529	962	208	82	1 045	10 962
2008–09	3 594	2 595	2 323	1 683	1 046	222	100	1 064	12 496
2009–10	4 672	2 659	2 775	1 974	1 063	307	163	783	14 251

Source: AIHW 2011b

Table A5.13 Disability support services users, by service type use and Indigenous status, Australia, 2009–10

	Indigenous		Non-Indigenous		Not stated/ not collected		Total	
	No.	%	No.	%	No.	%	No.	%
Accommodation support	1 937	13.6	36 203	13.7	1 714	10.4	39 854	13.5
Community support	7 705	54.1	112 564	42.6	7 640	46.5	127 909	43.4
Community access	2 169	15.2	50 583	19.1	5 880	35.8	58 632	19.9
Respite	2 163	15.2	31 569	11.9	2 246	13.7	35 978	12.2
Employment	4 883	34.3	113 578	43.0	340	2.1	118 801	40.3
Total	14 251	100.0	264 331	100.0	16 442	100.0	295 024	100.0

Source: AIHW 2011b

Table A5.14 Non-Indigenous disability support service users, all ages, States and Territories, Australia, 2005–06 to 2009–10

	NSW	Vic	Qld	WA	SA	Tas	ACT	NT	Australia
2005–06	478 60	64 727	28 270	18 282	19 212	5 291	3 082	853	186 805
2006–07	52 348	74 546	30 734	22 755	20 565	5 288	4 173	928	210 697
2007–08	57 377	77 569	33 403	19 647	23 175	5 773	4 358	1 320	221 638
2008–09	68 454	86 483	37 637	19 801	25 459	6 512	4 688	952	249 225
2009–10	76 407	87 298	40 236	20 513	27 316	7 883	4 905	766	264 331

Source: AIHW 2011b

Table A5.15 Disability support services users, aged 0–64 years by service type use and Indigenous status, Australia, 2009–10[a]

Service type	Indigenous users as a percentage of all service type users (%)	Usage rate among Indigenous service users (%)	Usage rate among non-indigenous users (%)	Usage rates among not stated users (%)	Total users for service type
Accommodation support					
Residential institutions, hostels and group homes	4.0	5.0	6.3	1.7	17 619
Personal care and in-home support	5.4	8.4	7.4	8.4	22 121
Alternative family placement and other accommodation support	7.1	0.9	0.6	0.4	1 807
Community support					
Therapy support	5.2	11.8	10.4	17.6	32 196
Early childhood intervention	5.3	8.9	8.3	5.3	24 149
Regional resource teams	7.2	11.2	7.5	2.5	21 926
Case management	6.4	29.4	21.6	25.7	65 413
Behaviour/specialist intervention, counselling and other community support	6.2	6.7	5.3	1.8	15 334
Community access					
Learning/life skills development	4.1	12.0	14.1	16.6	41 610
Recreation/holiday programs and other community access	2.9	4.1	6.2	19.3	20 058
Respite					
Centre-based respite	6.0	6.0	4.8	3.9	14 212
Flexible respite	6.4	9.5	7.0	7.7	21 175
Own home, host family and other respite	5.7	2.7	2.3	2.4	6 854
Employment					
Open employment	4.3	29.7	35.6	.	98 257
Supported and targeted employment	3.3	5.0	7.8	2.1	21 636
Total users	4.8	14 251	264 331	16 442	295 024

a. Service user data are estimates after use of a statistical linkage key to account for individuals who use more than one service. The term 'Indigenous' refers to service users who identified as Aboriginal or Torres Strait Islander people. Non-Indigenous refers to service users who reported not being of Aboriginal or Torres Strait Islander background.

Source: AIHW 2011b

Table A5.16 Indigenous disability support services users, by service type,

Australia, 2005–06 to 2009–10

Year	Accommodation support	Community support	Community access	Respite	Employment
2005–06	20.1	53.2	19.5	19.5	24.3
2006–07	20.4	55.4	18.6	18.9	23.6
2007–08	18.1	52.4	16.6	16.3	30.8
2008–09	16.1	66.8	17.3	19.4	32.9
2009–10	13.6	54.1	15.2	15.2	34.3

Source: AIHW 2011b

Table A5.17 Mean hours of support received by Indigenous status, service type and region, Australia, 2009–10

Service type and Indigenous status	Major cities	Inner regional	Outer regional	Remote/ very remote	Total[a]
Indigenous					
Accomodation support[b]	38.7	37.2	48.0	44.2	40.7
Community support[c]	1.2	1.7	0.8	1.0	1.2
Community access[d]	14.2	14.3	13.4	11.6	13.9
Respite	8.9	8.8	8.4	6.7	8.5
Employment	n.a.	n.a.	n.a.	n.a.	n.a.
Total services[e]	10.9	10.6	12.2	5.5	13.3
Non-Indigenous					
Accomodation support[b]	26.4	26.8	26.0	29.8	26.4
Community support[c]	1.4	1.4	0.7	0.6	1.3
Community access[d]	14.9	14.7	14.1	10.5	14.8
Respite	8.5	8.5	8.0	8.5	8.5
Employment	n.a.	n.a.	n.a.	n.a.	n.a.
Total services[e]	10.4	10.6	8.6	5.4	12.8

a. Includes service users who received zero hours of support from the service type category during the reference week, but excludes service users where the number of hours of support received from the service type category during the reference week was missing.

b. Includes attendant care/personal care; in-home accommodation support; and alternative family placement.

c. Includes case management, local coordination and development.

d. Excludes recreation/holiday programs.

e. Total of selected service type categories.

Source: AIHW 2011b

Table A5.18 Characteristics of users of disability support services, by Indigenous status, Australia, 2009–10

Service user characteristic	Indigenous		Non-Indigenous		Not stated/ not collected		Total	
	No.	%	No.	%	No.	%	No.	%
	Main income source (ages 16 +)							
Disability Support Pension	6 301	60.1	119 043	56.4	1 423	11.3	126 767	54.2
Other pension/benefit	2 298	21.9	40 535	19.2	152	1.2	42 985	18.4
Paid employment	531	5.1	17 759	8.4	63	0.5	18 353	7.8
Compensation payments	34	0.3	474	0.2	7	0.1	515	0.2
Other income	78	0.7	3 370	1.6	17	0.1	3 465	1.5
No income	368	3.5	5 587	2.6	27	0.2	5 982	2.6
Not known/not stated/ not collected	880	8.4	24 150	11.4	10 922	86.6	35 952	15.4
Total	10 490	100.0	210 918	100.0	12 611	100.0	234 019	100.0
	Labour force status (ages 15 +)							
Employed	2 114	19.7	60 437	28.3	525	4.1	63 076	26.6
Unemployed	4 021	37.5	73 856	34.6	345	2.7	78 222	33.0
Not in the labour force	3 949	36.9	63 372	29.6	1 104	8.6	68 425	28.8
Not stated	629	5.9	15 375	7.2	9 899	76.9	25 903	10.9
Not collected (recreation/holiday programs)	n.p.	–	720	0.3	1 000	7.8	1 722	0.7
Total	10 715	100.0	213 760	100.0	12 873	100.0	237 348	100.0

a. Service user data are estimates after use of a statistical linkage key to account for individuals who received services from more than one service type outlet during the 12-month period.

b. Row totals may not be the sum of components because service users may have accessed services in more than one State/Territory.

c. Service user data were not collected for all NDA service types (see Appendix 4 for details).

d. Service types 6.01–6.05 and 7.01–7.04 did not collect service user data, and so are excluded from this table.

e. n.p. = Not provided.

Source: AIHW 2011b

Table A5.19 Disability services users, aged 0–64 years per 1 000 potential population, by Indigenous status and State/Territory, Australia, 2005–06 to 2009–10

	NSW	Vic	Qld	WA	SA	Tas	ACT	NT	Australia
					2005–06				
Service users (all ages)									
Indigenous	1 709	1 795	1 433	1 045	634	168	42	410	7 182
Non-Indigenous	47 860	64 727	28 270	18 282	19 212	5 291	3 082	853	186 805
Not stated/not collected	1 564	14 431	1 101	4 715	761	257	203	126	23 156
Total	51 133	80 953	30 804	24 042	20 607	5 716	3 327	1 389	217 143
Service users (age 0–64 years)									
Indigenous	1 694	1 743	1 421	1 027	624	168	42	367	7 032
Non-Indigenous	46 559	60 283	27 491	17 816	16 642	5 153	3 063	780	177 018
Not stated/not collected	1 466	13 459	1 081	1 749	729	243	202	126	19 053
Total	49 719	75 485	29 993	20 592	17 995	5 564	3 307	1 273	203 103
Potential population (0–64 years)									
Indigenous	12 332	2 810	7 930	4 469	1 778	1 230	323	3 103	33 975
Non-Indigenous	220 820	170 928	132 559	66 643	51 750	15 893	11 291	4 438	674 321
Service users per 1 000 potential population (0–64 years)									
Indigenous	137.4	620.3	179.2	229.8	351.0	136.6	129.9	118.3	207.0
Non-Indigenous	210.8	352.7	207.4	267.3	321.6	324.2	271.3	175.8	262.5
					2006–07				
Service users (all ages)									
Indigenous	2 129	2 154	1 568	1 483	695	165	61	525	8 735
Non-Indigenous	52 348	74 546	30 734	22 755	20 565	5 288	4 173	928	210 697
Not stated/not collected	1 581	8 806	849	294	945	208	50	89	12 821
Total	56 058	85 506	33 151	24 532	22 205	5 661	4 284	1 542	232 253
Service users (age 0–64 years)									
Indigenous	2 102	2 089	1 553	1 471	682	162	61	455	8 530
Non-Indigenous	50 937	69 523	29 893	22 265	17 855	5 139	4 150	864	199 988
Not stated/not collected	1 455	7 566	825	230	868	201	50	88	11 282
Total	54 494	79 178	32 271	23 966	19 405	5 502	4 261	1 407	219 800

	NSW	Vic	Qld	WA	SA	Tas	ACT	NT	Australia
Potential population (0–64 years)									
Indigenous	12 640	2 877	8 170	4 587	1 817	1 261	333	3 192	34 877
Non-Indigenous	223 176	173 873	135 968	68 175	52 427	16 050	11 426	4 522	685 616
Service users per 1 000 potential population (0–64 years)									
Indigenous	166.3	726.0	190.1	320.7	375.3	128.5	183.2	142.6	244.6
Non-Indigenous	228.2	399.8	219.9	326.6	340.6	320.2	363.2	191.1	291.7
2007–08									
Service users (all ages)									
Indigenous	2 882	2 323	2 143	1 529	962	208	82	1 045	10 962
Non-Indigenous	57 377	77 569	33 403	19 647	23 175	5 773	4 358	1 320	221 638
Not stated/not collected	1 604	9 420	1 023	143	1 126	163	89	115	13 681
Total	61 863	89 312	36 569	21 319	25 263	6 144	4 529	2 480	246 281
Service users (age 0–64 years)									
Indigenous	2 860	2 240	2 125	1 491	945	205	82	890	10 633
Non-Indigenous	56 171	72 951	32 616	19 175	20 391	5 583	4 336	1 153	211 394
Not stated/not collected	1 528	8 152	996	137	1 038	153	89	111	12 202
Total	60 559	83 343	35 737	20 803	22 374	5 941	4 507	2 154	234 229
Potential population (0–64 years)									
Indigenous	12 912	2 953	8 434	4 703	1 860	1 293	340	3 277	35 772
Non-Indigenous	226 156	177 077	139 399	69 929	53 081	16 191	16 527	4 590	702 948
Service users per 1 000 potential population (0–64 years)									
Indigenous	221.5	758.6	252.0	317.0	508.1	158.5	241.2	271.6	297.2
Non-Indigenous	248.4	412.0	234.0	274.2	384.1	344.8	262.4	251.2	300.7
2008–09									
Service users (all ages)									
Indigenous	3 594	2 595	2 323	1 683	1 046	222	100	1 064	12 496
Non-Indigenous	68 454	86 483	37 637	19 801	25 459	6 512	4 688	952	249 225
Not stated/not collected	2 117	12 514	1 445	137	913	178	140	137	17 580
Total	74 165	101 592	41 405	21 621	27 418	6 912	4 928	2 153	279 301

	NSW	Vic	Qld	WA	SA	Tas	ACT	NT	Australia
Service users (age 0–64 years)									
Indigenous	3 556	2 473	2 297	1 657	1 020	217	100	876	12 066
Non-Indigenous	66 360	78 348	36 860	19 346	22 531	6 318	4 661	834	234 503
Not stated/not collected	2 015	8 849	1 414	137	840	166	140	136	13 696
Total	71 931	89 670	40 571	21 140	24 391	6 701	4 901	1 846	260 265
Potential population (0–64 years)									
Indigenous	11 818	2 692	7 760	4 290	1 710	1 192	308	2 985	32 757
Non-Indigenous	207 059	162 616	129 021	64 882	48 472	14 809	10 616	4 261	641 735
Service users per 1 000 potential population (0–64 years)									
Indigenous	300.9	918.5	296.0	386.3	596.4	182.0	324.2	293.5	368.4
Non-Indigenous	320.5	481.8	285.7	298.2	464.8	426.6	439.1	195.7	365.4
2009–10									
Service users (all ages)									
Indigenous	4 672	2 659	2 775	1 974	1 063	307	163	783	14 251
Non-Indigenous	76 407	87 298	40 236	20 513	27 316	7 883	4 905	766	264 331
Not stated/not collected	2,322	11 699	1 036	231	632	252	152	120	16,442
Total	83 401	101 656	44 047	22 718	29 011	8 442	5 220	1 669	295 024
Service users (0–64 years)									
Indigenous	4 631	2 557	2 750	1 925	1 030	303	163	657	13 873
Non-Indigenous	74 251	79 551	39 451	20 052	24 040	7 674	4 877	686	249 594
Not stated/not collected	2 237	9 026	1 014	222	540	243	152	119	13 551
Total	81 119	91 134	43 215	22 199	25 610	8 220	5 192	1 462	277 018
Potential population (0–64 years)									
Indigenous	12 054	2 758	7 997	4 400	1 754	1 218	317	3 068	33 566
Non-Indigenous	209 901	165 839	132 019	66 715	49 015	14 936	10 781	4 363	653 569
Service users per 1 000 potential population (0–64 years)									
Indigenous	384.2	927.1	343.9	437.5	587.2	248.8	514.2	214.1	413.3
Non-Indigenous	353.7	479.7	298.8	300.6	490.5	513.8	452.4	157.2	381.9

a. Service user data are estimates after use of a statistical linkage key to account for individuals who received services from more than one service type outlet during the 12-month period. Totals for Australia may not be the sum of components because individuals may have accessed services in more than one State or territory during the 12-month period.

b. In tables the term 'Indigenous' refers to service users who identified as Aboriginal and/or Torres Strait Islander people. 'Non-Indigenous' refers to service users who reported not being of Aboriginal or Torres Strait Islander background.

c. Indigenous potential population estimates are experimental.

d. Indigenous potential population estimates are calculated by applying Indigenous/non-Indigenous sex and 10-year age group rates of severe/profound disability in each State/Territory to Indigenous and non-Indigenous population data in each State/Territory by sex and 10-year age group for people aged 0–64.

e. Indigenous population figures are based on revised ABS Series B projections of the Indigenous population by State/territory for June 2008 (ABS 2009a).

Source: AIHW analysis of CSTDA NMDS 2007–08, 2008–09; DS NMDS 2009–10, ABS 2009a

Table A5.20 Indigenous potential population aged 0–64 years accessing State/Territory disability support services, by remoteness area, Australia, 2009–10[a]

	2005–06	2006–07	2007–08	2008–09	2009–10
Major cities	133.7	168	185.7	241.9	284.9
Inner Regional	231.1	285	347.9	436.0	508.6
Outer Regional/Remote/ Very Remote	362.9	379	525.1	609.9	626.0
Total[b]	207.0	245	297.2	368.4	413.3

a. Service user data are estimates after use of a statistical linkage key to account for individuals who received services from more than one service type outlet during the 12-month period. Total service users may not be the sum of service group components because individuals may have accessed more than one service group over the 12-month period. Includes service users whose remoteness area is unknown (service user postcodes provided by all services attended were not stated or not collected.

b. Rate are calculated per 1 000 using the potential population of Indigenous persons aged 0–64 years.

Source: AIHW (unpublished) DS NMDS 2009–10; AIHW analysis of the ABS Indigenous Projected Population 2009; 2009 Survey of Disability, Ageing and Carers; and 2006 Census of Population and Housing (National Disability Agreement Attachment tables)

Table A5.21 Problems accessing services, Indigenous persons aged 15 years and over, by remoteness, Australia, 2008

	Profound/severe and unspecified limitation			No disability or long-term health condition		
	Remote	Non-remote	Total	Remote	Non-remote	Total
Whether had problems accessing services	Per cent			Per cent		
Had problems accessing services	46.1	32.4	35.8	38.0	19.4	24.1
Did not have problems accessing services	53.9	67.6	64.2	62.0	80.6	75.9
Total	100.0	100.0	100.0	100.0	100.0	100.0
Types of selected services has problems accessing						
ATSI health workers	6.5	7.3	7.1	5.0	3.8	4.1
Dentists	30.5	21.4	23.6	24.5	12.5	15.5
Doctors	13.6	11.0	11.6	11.1	6.3	7.5
Other health workers	5.5	3.2	3.8	2.9	0.9	1.4
Hospitals	17.6	5.9	8.7	11.5	2.1	4.5
Legal services	10.0	6.0	7.0	8.0	2.7	4.0
Employment services	5.8	4.1	4.5	5.7	1.8	2.8
Phone companies	7.4	3.0	4.1	5.1	1.9	2.7
Centrelink	10.3	7.2	8.0	6.9	3.0	4.0
Banks and other financial places	14.1	3.7	6.2	8.7	1.2	3.1
Medicare	4.2	2.5	2.9	3.3	0.8	1.4
Mental health services	6.4	4.2	4.8	4.7	1.3	2.2
Other services	0.8	0.9	0.9	0.3	0.2	0.2
No problems	53.9	67.6	64.2	62.0	80.6	75.9
Type of barrier to accessing any services						
Transport / Distance	20.7	9.1	11.9	16.8	3.8	7.1
Cost of service	7.7	12.4	11.2	5.5	6.9	6.5
No services in the area	24.8	8.7	12.6	22.7	6.2	10.4
Not enough services in the area	23.4	11.4	14.3	17.7	6.1	9.1
Waiting time too long or not available at time required	19.5	18.1	18.4	12.5	10.8	11.2
Services not culturally appropriate	2.8	3.2	3.1	2.1	1.4	1.5
Don't trust services	4.1	4.6	4.4	2.5	1.5	1.8
Treated badly / Discrimination	2.0	1.9	1.9	0.8	0.7	0.7
Other	2.1	5.3	4.5	1.2	2.4	2.1
Did not have problems accessing services	53.9	67.6	64.2	62.0	80.6	75.9
Total	100.0	100.0	100.0	100.0	100.0	100.0
Total number	39 746	123 198	162 944	41 755	122 402	164 157

Source: AIHW analysis of 2008 NATSISS (unpublished)

Table A5.22 Indigenous persons who did not access health services when needed and why, by remoteness, Australia, 2004–05

	Non-remote %	Remote %	Total %
Whether needed to go to dentist in last 12 months, but didn't[a]			
Yes	23	16	21
No	77	84	79
Total persons[b]	331 272	121 086	452 358
Reasons didn't go to a dentist			
Cost	32	15	29
Too busy (including work, personal or family responsibilities)	15	11	14
Dislikes (service/professional/afraid /embarrassed)	21	20	21
Waiting time too long or not available at time required	21	23	22
Decided not to seek care	14	8	13
Transport/distance	7	28	11
Not available in area	3	28	8
Felt it would be inadequate	2[c]	2[d]	2[c]
Discrimination/ not culturally appropriate/ language problems	—[d]	1[d]	—[c]
Other	9	7[c]	8
Total who needed to visit dentist, but didn't[b]	74 062	18 871	92 933
Whether needed to visit doctor in last 12 months, but didn't			
Yes	17	10	15
No	83	90	85
Total persons[b]	348 315	125 995	474 310
Reasons why didn't visit the doctor when needed to			
Cost	14	4[c]	12
Too busy (including work, personal or family responsibilities)	26	17	24
Dislikes (service/professional/ afraid/embarrassed)	10	11	10
Waiting time too long or not available at time required	14	15	14
Decided not to seek care	27	22	26
Transport/distance	11	28[c]	14
Not available in area	2[d]	13[c]	4[c]
Felt it would be inadequate	5	7[c]	5

	Non-remote %	Remote %	Total %
Discrimination/ not culturally appropriate/ language problems	1	1[d]	1[c]
Other	12	5	11
Total who needed to visit doctor, but didn't[b]	57 653	12 012	69 665
Whether needed to go to other health professional in last 12 months, but didn't,			
Yes	9	5	8
No	91	95	92
Total persons[b]	348 315	125 995	474 310
Why didn't go to other health professional (OHP)			
Cost	33	5[d]	28
Too busy (including work, personal or family responsibilities)	27	20	26
Dislikes (service/professional/ afraid/embarrassed)	12	11[c]	12
Waiting time too long or not available at time required	7[c]	19	9
Decided not to seek care	18	16	17
Transport/distance	7[c]	15[c]	8
Not available in area	2[c]	30	7
Felt it would be inadequate	5[c]	5[d]	5
Discrimination/ not culturally appropriate/ language problems	2[d]	2[d]	*2
Other	11	10[c]	11
Total who needed to visit OHP but didn't[b]	29 699	5 971	35 670
Whether needed to go to hospital in the last 12 months, but didn't,			
Yes	7	7	7
No	93	93	93
Total persons[b]	348 315	125 995	474 310
Why didn't visit hospital			
Cost	5[c]	3[c]	4
Too busy (including work, personal or family responsibilities)	17	16	16
Dislikes (service/professional/ afraid/embarrassed)	18	9[c]	16
Waiting time too long or not available at time required	18	10[c]	16
Decided not to seek care	25	26	25

	Non-remote %	Remote %	Total %
Transport/distance	13	34	19
Not available in area	2[c]	8[c]	4[c]
Felt it would be inadequate	6	7[c]	6
Discrimination/ not culturally appropriate/ language problems	2[c]	2[d]	2[c]
Other	15	9	14
Total who needed to visit hospital, but didn't[b]	22 982	8 840	31 822

a. Persons aged 2 years and over.

b. Total includes 'not stated'.

c. Estimate has a relative standard error between 25% and 50% and should be used with caution.

d. Estimate has a relative standard error greater than 50% and is considered too unreliable for general use.

Source: AIHW 2011a

CAEPR Research Monograph Series

1. *Aborigines in the Economy: A Select Annotated Bibliography of Policy Relevant Research 1985–90*, L. M. Allen, J. C. Altman, and E. Owen (with assistance from W. S. Arthur), 1991.

2. *Aboriginal Employment Equity by the Year 2000*, J. C. Altman (ed.), published for the Academy of Social Sciences in Australia, 1991.

3. *A National Survey of Indigenous Australians: Options and Implications*, J. C. Altman (ed.), 1992.

4. *Indigenous Australians in the Economy: Abstracts of Research, 1991–92*, L. M. Roach and K. A. Probst, 1993.

5. *The Relative Economic Status of Indigenous Australians, 1986–91*, J. Taylor, 1993.

6. *Regional Change in the Economic Status of Indigenous Australians, 1986–91*, J. Taylor, 1993.

7. *Mabo and Native Title: Origins and Institutional Implications*, W. Sanders (ed.), 1994.

8. *The Housing Need of Indigenous Australians, 1991*, R. Jones, 1994.

9. *Indigenous Australians in the Economy: Abstracts of Research, 1993–94*, L. M. Roach and H. J. Bek, 1995.

10. *The Native Title Era: Emerging Issues for Research, Policy, and Practice*, J. Finlayson and D. E. Smith (eds), 1995.

11. *The 1994 National Aboriginal and Torres Strait Islander Survey: Findings and Future Prospects*, J. C. Altman and J. Taylor (eds), 1996.

12. *Fighting Over Country: Anthropological Perspectives*, D. E. Smith and J. Finlayson (eds), 1997.

13. *Connections in Native Title: Genealogies, Kinship, and Groups*, J. D. Finlayson, B. Rigsby, and H. J. Bek (eds), 1999.

14. *Land Rights at Risk? Evaluations of the Reeves Report*, J. C. Altman, F. Morphy, and T. Rowse (eds), 1999.

15. *Unemployment Payments, the Activity Test, and Indigenous Australians: Understanding Breach Rates*, W. Sanders, 1999.

16. *Why Only One in Three? The Complex Reasons for Low Indigenous School Retention*, R. G. Schwab, 1999.

17. *Indigenous Families and the Welfare System: Two Community Case Studies*, D. E. Smith (ed.), 2000.

18. *Ngukurr at the Millennium: A Baseline Profile for Social Impact Planning in South-East Arnhem Land*, J. Taylor, J. Bern, and K. A. Senior, 2000.

19. *Aboriginal Nutrition and the Nyirranggulung Health Strategy in Jawoyn Country*, J. Taylor and N. Westbury, 2000.

20. *The Indigenous Welfare Economy and the CDEP Scheme*, F. Morphy and W. Sanders (eds), 2001.

21. *Health Expenditure, Income and Health Status among Indigenous and Other Australians*, M. C. Gray, B. H. Hunter, and J. Taylor, 2002.

22. *Making Sense of the Census: Observations of the 2001 Enumeration in Remote Aboriginal Australia*, D. F. Martin, F. Morphy, W. G. Sanders and J. Taylor, 2002.

23. *Aboriginal Population Profiles for Development Planning in the Northern East Kimberley*, J. Taylor, 2003.

24. *Social Indicators for Aboriginal Governance: Insights from the Thamarrurr Region, Northern Territory*, J. Taylor, 2004.

25. *Indigenous People and the Pilbara Mining Boom: A Baseline for Regional Participation*, J. Taylor and B. Scambary, 2005.

26. *Assessing the Evidence on Indigenous Socioeconomic Outcomes: A Focus on the 2002 NATSISS*, B. H. Hunter (ed.), 2006.

27. *The Social Effects of Native Title: Recognition, Translation, Coexistence*, B. R. Smith and F. Morphy (eds), 2007.

28. *Agency, Contingency and Census Process: Observations of the 2006 Indigenous Enumeration Strategy in remote Aboriginal Australia*, F. Morphy (ed.), 2008.

29. *Contested Governance: Culture, Power and Institutions in Indigenous Australia*, J. Hunt, D. Smith, S. Garling and W. Sanders (eds), 2008.

30. *Power, Culture, Economy: Indigenous Australians and Mining*, J. Altman and D. Martin (eds), 2009.

31. *Demographic and Socioeconomic Outcomes Across the Indigenous Australian Lifecourse*, N. Biddle and M. Yap, 2010.

32. *Survey Analysis for Indigenous Policy in Australia: Social Science Perspectives*, B. Hunter and N. Biddle (eds), 2012.

33. *My Country, Mine Country: Indigenous People, Mining and Development Contestation in Remote Australia*, B. Scambary, 2013.

Centre for Aboriginal Economic Policy Research,
College of Arts and Social Sciences,
The Australian National University, Canberra, ACT, 0200

Information on CAEPR Discussion Papers, Working Papers and Research Monographs (Nos 1-19) and abstracts and summaries of all CAEPR print publications and those published electronically can be found at the following WWW address: http://caepr.anu.edu.au

www.ingramcontent.com/pod-product-compliance
Lightning Source LLC
Chambersburg PA
CBHW061227270326
41928CB00025B/3435